The
100 BEST
Great Lakes
SHIPWRECKS

Volume II

Lake Michigan, Lake Superior

Books by Cris Kohl:

DIVE SOUTHWESTERN ONTARIO!

SHIPWRECK TALES: THE ST. CLAIR RIVER (TO 1900)

DIVE ONTARIO! THE GUIDE TO SHIPWRECKS AND SCUBA DIVING

DIVE ONTARIO TWO! MORE ONTARIO SHIPWRECK STORIES

TREACHEROUS WATERS: KINGSTON'S SHIPWRECKS

THE 100 BEST GREAT LAKES SHIPWRECKS, VOLUME I

THE 100 BEST GREAT LAKES SHIPWRECKS, VOLUME II

The
100 BEST
Great Lakes

SHIPWRECKS

Volume II

Lake Michigan, Lake Superior

by *Cris Kohl*

ILLUSTRATED WITH PHOTOGRAPHS,
MAPS, AND DRAWINGS

THE 100 BEST GREAT LAKES SHIPWRECKS, VOLUME II

COPYRIGHT © 1998 BY SEAWOLF COMMUNICATIONS, INC.

ALL RIGHTS RESERVED

ISBN 0-9681437-3-3

LIBRARY OF CONGRESS CARD CATALOG NUMBER: 98-90679

Published by
SEAWOLF COMMUNICATIONS, INC.,
P.O. BOX 66,
WEST CHICAGO, IL 60186
U.S.A.

DISCLAIMER: Although the author and publisher have tried to make the information as accurate as possible, they accept no responsibility for any loss, injury, death, or inconvenience sustained by any person using this book.

NOTE: Photo credits are shown in terms of the author's source for the photograph rather than a specific photographer who might have taken it, except where the photographer is known and specifically named. Photos © photographers as indicated (excluding Cris Kohl). Artwork © artists as indicated. Text, maps of the individual Great Lakes, and Cris Kohl photos © Seawolf Communications, Inc.

Printed in Hong Kong

FIRST EDITION: NOVEMBER, 1998

03 02 01 00   5 4 3 2

COVER PHOTOGRAPH: *Decoratively draped in languid arcs and straight lines like an iron curtain in a fluid world, the bow chains from the steamer,* MYRON, *in about 50' of Lake Superior water off Whitefish Point, Michigan, tumble off the collapsed wooden deck and disappear into the shifting sands in an artistic pose.*   PHOTO BY CRIS KOHL.

DEDICATION

TO JOAN FORSBERG---

THE BEST PARTNER

ACKNOWLEDGEMENTS

The author sincerely thanks the following individuals and organizations, listed alphabetically, for their assistance during the writing of this book:

INDIVIDUALS: Josh Barnes of Charlevoix, MI; Kent Bellrichard of Milwaukee, WI; James Brotz of Sheboygan, WI; Steve Carrigan of Aurora, IL; Dale Currier of Oswego, NY; Dr. Roger Dean of Port Sanilac, MI; Don Edwards of Thunder Bay, ON; Paul Ehorn of Elgin, IL; Dr. Gary Elliott of Madison Heights, MI; Darryl Ertel of Flint, MI; Tom Farnquist of Sault Ste. Marie, MI; Chuck & Jeri Feltner of Drummond Island and Dearborn, MI; Joan Forsberg of High Lake, IL; Gary Gentile of Philadelphia, PA; Robert Graham of the Center for Archival Collections, Bowling Green State University, Ohio; Capt. Jerry Guyer of Milwaukee, WI; Dennis Hale of Dayton, OH; Joyce Hayward of Bellevue, OH; Adam Henley of Ajax, ON; Captain Jim Herbert of Barcelona, NY; Capt. Bill Hoey of Detroit, MI; Capt. Jim Jackman of Calumet, MI; Tim Juhl of Carsonville, MI; C. Patrick Labadie, curator, Canal Park Museum, Duluth, MN; Dani Lee of Montreal, Quebec; Daniel Lenihan, Principal Investigator, National Park Service, Submerged Cultural Resources Unit, Santa Fe, New Mexico; Capt. Peter Lindquist of Munising, MI; Barb & Ian Marshall of Stevensville, ON; Marcy McElmon of Trenton, ON; Robert McGreevy of Grosse Point Woods, MI; David & Sue Millhouser of Cape Ann, Massachusetts; Valerie Olson-van Heest of Holland, MI; David Ostifichuk of Smiths Falls, ON; Doug Pettingill of Picton, ON; Capt. Roy Pickering of Blenheim, ON; Steve Radovan of Sheboygan, WI; Tom Rasbeck of Oswego, NY; Peter Rindlisbacher of Amherstburg, ON; Ralph Roberts of Saginaw, MI; Spencer Shonicker of Kingston, ON; Mark Standfield of Toronto, ON, for initially planting the idea for a book like this into my head; Capt. Jim and Pat Stayer of Lexington, MI; John Steele of Waukegan, IL; Frederick Stonehouse of Marquette, MI; James Taylor of Picton, ON; Peter Tomasino of St. Charles, IL; David Trotter of Canton, MI; Frank Troxell of Davisburg, MI; Sharon Troxell of White Lake Twp, MI; Matt Turchi of Flint, MI; Rev. Peter van der Linden, Marysville, MI; Georgann & Michael Wachter of Avon Lake, OH; George West of Sheboygan, WI; Erika Wetzel, of Windsor, ON; Paul Woehrmann of the Milwaukee Public Library, WI; Susan Yankoo & George Wheeler of Point Traverse, ON; Jon Zeaman of Milwaukee, WI; and Dean Ziegler of Bloomville, OH.

ORGANIZATIONS AND THEIR HELPFUL STAFFS: The Center for Archival Collections (formerly the Institute for Great Lakes Research) Bowling Green State University, OH; the Great Lakes Historical Society, Vermilion, OH; the Great Lakes Marine Collection of the Milwaukee Public Library/the Wisconsin Marine Historical Society, Milwaukee, WI; the Lake Carriers' Association, Cleveland, OH; the Marine Museum of the Great Lakes at Kingston, Ontario; the Metropolitan Toronto Public Library, ON; and the U.S. National Park Service, Submerged Cultural Resources Unit, Santa Fe, New Mexico.

Special thanks to David Bondy for holding the fort while I chased the rainbows.

I apologize to anyone I may have inadvertently overlooked. Finally, I wish to acknowledge and thank the people who have read my previous books and magazine articles on the Great Lakes, and especially to those many who took the trouble to write to me some of the most interesting, informative, and inspiring letters that I have ever read.

CONTENTS

VOLUME I CONTAINS:

FOREWORD

TO VOLUME II

by
C. Patrick Labadie

CURATOR,
CANAL PARK VISITOR CENTER & MARINE MUSEUM,
U.S. ARMY CORPS OF ENGINEERS,
DULUTH, MINNESOTA

The Great Lakes of North America are one of the natural wonders of the world, as anyone knows who lives by their shores or vacations on their blue waters. They're the largest store of fresh water on earth; they encompass several different ecosystems which are as fragile as they are breathtakingly beautiful; and they have the capacity to open the very heartland of America to deepwater ships.

Their physical attributes aside, the Great Lakes also have a colorful and romantic history which sets them apart as a distinct cultural region. The Lakes bind together the several states and provinces of two great nations, bringing under one geographical umbrella literally scores of large industrial cities and tens of millions of people...all "citizens of the Great Lakes."

Author Cris Kohl pays tribute to the Great Lakes in his two-volume *The 100 Best Great Lakes Shipwrecks*. In particular, he explores one of the Lakes' most colorful and most endangered resources, the shipwrecks which dot their bottomlands.

Kohl's previous books on Great Lakes shipwrecks have won him the well-deserved recognition of the diving community, but this two-volume set is geared for a wider audience, with a good overview of the region's history and much more descriptive information about the ships.

For the diver and non-diver alike, here is an assessment of the finest examples of submerged cultural resources in the Great Lakes. It will bring to life for the larger public the same magic enjoyed by diving veterans around these Inland Seas.

C. Patrick Labadie
Duluth, Minnesota,
July, 1998

INTRODUCTION

Five immense bodies of fresh water form a unique and highly conspicuous natural feature near the middle of the North American continent. Known collectively and historically as the Great Lakes, a deserved appellation not the least bit guilty of exaggeration, these vast entities of water --- Lakes Ontario, Erie, Huron, Michigan, and Superior --- have a combined area of 94,560 square miles, making them the largest surface of fresh water in the world.

The Great Lakes region, running 860 miles in an east-west direction and 690 miles in a north-south direction, covers an area larger than France.

Geographically, the Great Lakes drain from west to east, emptying eventually through the St. Lawrence River into the Atlantic Ocean. Lake Superior lies at an altitude of 600 feet above sea level; Lakes Michigan and Huron are at the same 579-foot level; Lake Erie sits at 570 feet above sea level, while Lake Ontario, after the waters' dramatic drop over Niagara Falls as it enters this lake, rests at 245 feet above sea level.

Lake	Area in sq. mi.	World rank	Max. depth	Vol. in cu. mi.	World rank
Ontario	7,840	14th	802'	393	11th
Erie	9,910	11th	210'	116	15th
Huron	23,000	5th	750'	849	7th
Michigan	22,300	6th	923'	1,180	6th
Superior	31,700	2nd	1,333'	2,935	4th

Politically, the five Great Lakes are shared by eight U. S. states (east to west: New York, Pennsylvania, Ohio, Michigan, Indiana, Illinois, Wisconsin, and Minnesota), and one Canadian province (Ontario). About 60% of the Great Lakes surface waters lie within the United States, while approximately 40% are contained within Canada. Lake Michigan is the only one of the Great Lakes lying totally within the United States.

Environmentally, all the Great Lakes except Superior have witnessed increased concentrations of most chemicals since the year 1900. Lakes Ontario, Erie, and Michigan have suffered a four-fold increase of chloride, sodium, and sulfate in that time span, while Lake Erie's nitrogen content has increased five times what it was in 1900 and its phosphorus level tripled between 1945 and 1975. These components are significant because they stimulate algae and zebra mussel growth which, for scuba divers, affect visibility and aesthetics with regards to shipwreck exploration. What these elements do to the overall scheme of things in the Great Lakes is even more devastating.

Lake	Max. depth	Mean depth	Length in miles	Width in miles	Retention time of water
Ontario	802'	283'	193	53	8 years
Erie	210'	58'	241	57	3 years
Huron	750'	195'	206	101	20-22 years
Michigan	923'	276'	321	118	90-100 years
Superior	1,333'	487'	383	160	110-190 years

Environmentally, humans as a species have acted unthinkingly about the Great Lakes' future. Atlantic salmon were once naturally plentiful in these waters, but the polluting and damming of rivers which flow into these lakes caused their extinction by 1880. Whitefish, once thriving in huge numbers, were seriously restricted by the late 1800's for the same reasons. Great Lakes sturgeon were greedily overfished and are now on the edge of extinction. Introduced into the Great Lakes were carp, smelt, sea lamprey, alewives, zebra mussels, and the ruffe, all originally foreign to these waters. On the other hand, lake trout and salmon have been re-introduced to the Great Lakes, with varying degrees of success. The struggle to maintain an acceptable balance is ongoing.

Historically, the Great Lakes provided the first means of easy transportation, with First Nation canoes and, later, European vessels plying these natural highways into the continent's heartland. The first of the lakes to be viewed by a European was Lake Huron in 1609 or 1610, when the French explorer, Étienne Brûlé, arrived. Brûlé and Samuel de Champlain are credited with being the first white men to visit Lake Ontario, in 1615. Brûlé and Grenoble reputedly were, in 1622, the first Europeans to see Lake Superior. In 1634, Jean Nicolet became the first white man to reach Lake Michigan, while much later, in 1669, the first European to gaze over Lake Erie was Louis Jolliet. Europeans quickly discovered this area's resource treasures, such as lumber, fertile farmland, freshwater, and minerals like coal, copper, iron, and limestone.

Surface area of the Great Lakes in square miles:

	Ontario	Erie	Huron	Michigan	Superior
Canada	3,880	4,930	13,900	none	11,100
United States	3,460	4,980	9,100	22,300	20,600
Boundary length:	174.6 mi	253 mi.	261 mi.	none	282.8 mi.

Industries and huge urban populations quickly developed because of these resources. In the year 1800, about 300,000 people lived in the Great Lakes region; in 1970, the population had risen to 37,000,000, an increase of 12,000%. Most of this dense, modern settlement extends from Milwaukee-Chicago around southern Lake Michigan, across to Detroit, then around the southern shore of Lake Erie through Toledo-Cleveland-Buffalo, culminating in the "Golden Horseshoe" area along western Lake Ontario running from Niagara Falls to Hamilton to Toronto in Canada.

This incredibly large megalopolis continues to place increasing pressures upon our limited Great Lakes resources, whether these be fresh water, lumber stands, mineral deposits, or the recreational exploration of shipwrecks.

Scuba diving is one activity which this book addresses. The cold, fresh waters of the Great Lakes yield no tropical characteristics, such as colorful coral and exotic fish, but they do contain the best preserved shipwrecks in the world!

That is a powerful, world-renowned claim, not to be taken lightly. A letter I received in 1988 from a marine museum curator in Fremantle, Western Australia, contained the statement, "I have, of course, heard about your amazingly well-preserved [Great Lakes] shipwrecks...." People in the rest of the world are aware that the "submerged cultural resources" in the Great Lakes are definitely unique. Unfortunately, some people in the Great Lakes take our shipwrecks for granted, stealing artifacts and depriving us of chances to view remnants of another era frozen in time in these underwater museums.

Historians surmise that, of the approximately 15,000 vessels that plied Great Lakes waters in recorded history, about 4,000 became permanent residents known as shipwrecks, numbers which always stymie and impress the imaginations of locals and visitors alike. That so much maritime commerce could be sustained on these inland seas in the middle of the North American continent is one of the least-known facts in the overall scheme of world history.

These facts should give an idea of the intense shipping traffic on the Great Lakes in earlier years:

- By 1845, there were 60 steamships and 270 sailing vessels on the Upper Great Lakes alone (that is, upstream of Niagara Falls, namely Lakes Erie, Huron, Michigan, and Superior).

- By 1860, there were over 1,450 commercial ships of all types plying the waters of the five Great Lakes.

- By 1870, there were over 2,000 commercial sailing ships listed on the Upper Great Lakes alone. This was the peak year for sailing vessels.

- In the year 1882, Chicago Harbor recorded 26,000 commercial vessel arrivals and clearances (departures).

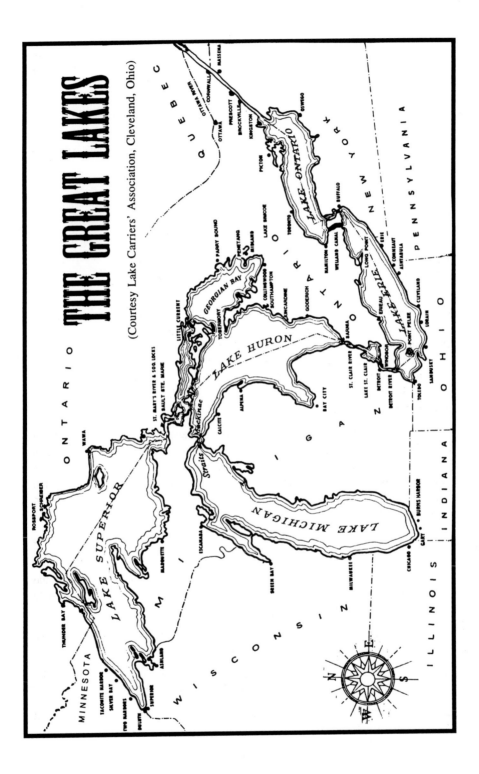

THE GREAT LAKES

(Courtesy Lake Carriers' Association, Cleveland, Ohio)

- One 1892 photograph of Harbor Beach, MI (on Lake Huron) shows 110 crowded commercial steamers, schooners, barges, and tugs taking refuge from a bad lake blow. Talk about tight rafting off!

- As late as 1916, there were 1,837 steamships and 162 sailing vessels working commercially on the Great Lakes.

With numbers like these, it is little wonder that many of these thousands of ships ended up on the bottom of our inland seas.

Fewer than half of these 4,000 shipwrecks have been located to date, but the rate of discovery is changing geometrically with refinements and cost reductions in electronic detection or positioning devices, such as sidescan sonar and the global positioning system. Since these natural shipwrecks in the Great Lakes are a limited, nonrenewable resource, what we have must be treated with the greatest of respect so we do not greedily devour or destroy these resources for the immediate gratification of our own generation's limited time frame.

These books will tell you about the 100 best shipwrecks in the Great Lakes. The criteria for establishing some idea of "bestness" were straightforward:

1. a maximum depth of 130', since this is the safe sport diving limit recommended by training agencies;

2. positive identification of the shipwreck. There are many excellent "mystery" shipwrecks in the Great Lakes, such as the coal schooner in Lake Erie off Port Stanley, Ontario, and numerous unidentified schooners in Lake Huron which have somehow ended up as highlights at scuba or shipwreck shows, but the true challenge lies in identifying them. Without a name, there can be no opportunity to research and appreciate that vessel's history;

3. intactness of the hull (does the shipwreck still look like a ship?);

4. the presence of nautical components or artifacts;

5. the reliability of fairly good underwater visibility at the site;

6. an acceptable lack of zebra mussel coverage of the shipwreck and its components.

That said, let me make it clear that these criteria were not "carved in granite." Had they been, shipwrecks in Lake Erie, lower Lake Michigan, and some parts of Lake Ontario would not have made the list simply because of their camouflaged condition due to cyclical zebra mussel encrustation, or steel ships that were dynamited and no longer have intact hulls, such as the *Sevona* or the *Mapledawn,* would have been eliminated in spite of their absolutely fascinating site characteristics. Also not taken into account in deciding "The 100 Best" were accessibility of the shipwreck (it didn't matter if it was a shore dive or well off shore), or the supposed degree of historical significance of the wreck (every shipwreck has a story to tell, and a valuable history).

Let me explain the headings found in the box that accompanies each shipwreck:

- VESSEL NAME: The was the ship's name at the time of sinking. The launching name is also given if it was different.

- RIG: This refers to the type of vessel it was at the time of loss (see Appendix A for "Vessel Types").

- DIMENSIONS: The first number represents the length of the vessel, followed by a number showing the ship's beam, followed by a number showing the vessel's draft, or depth. All numbers are in feet (represented by the symbol ') and inches (represented by the symbol "). All dimension figures given are those at the time of the ship's loss, since the vessel may have had major alterations or size-changing rebuilds in its history.

- LAUNCHED: Wherever possible, the exact date, as opposed to just giving the year in which a ship was launched, is given. This is for the sake of those researchers who may wish to delve into local archives in quest of contemporary accounts describing the ship's launching. This date is followed by the launch location.

- DATE LOST: This is the date that the ship sank, ending its active career on the Great Lakes and beginning its passive career as a scuba dive site.

- CAUSE OF LOSS: Ships sank for a number of reasons, mainly foundering (filling with water and sinking), burning, colliding (usually with another ship), stranding (running aground and often breaking up), exploding (boilers on steamships were notorious for this), scuttling (purposely being sunk to discard a vessel no longer considered useful), and abandoning.

- CARGO: The vast majority of Great Lakes vessels were workhorses which usually carried heavy loads of lumber, coal, iron ore, or grain. Sorry, no gold-and-silver-laden ships traversed these waters. "In ballast" means the ship carried no cargo at the time of sinking.

- LIVES LOST: This is the number of persons who perished when that ship sank. If known, the number of the entire crew is also given.

- LOCATION: This gives a very general idea of where that shipwreck is located, e.g. 4.5 miles off Milwaukee, WI.

- DEPTH: Once again, this is given in feet. If only one number is given, or the higher number of a range, is where the deepest part of that sunken vessel rests. Some shipwrecks rise 30' from the bottom!

- ACCESS: Most shipwrecks can be reached only by means of a boat; a few, however, are accessible from shore.

- DIVING SKILL LEVEL: Each shipwreck site is identified as suitable for novice, intermediate, or advanced divers, or midway points in between each of these designations. I thank Joyce Hayward and the Bay Area Divers of Ohio for their assistance in these categories:

A novice dive: a) is less than 60' in depth, b) is suitable for a newly-certified diver or infrequent diver, c) has no or very little current, d) has good visibility, e) may include shipwreck diving with no penetration.

An intermediate dive: a) is suitable for more experienced divers, b) may reach depths between 60' and 100', c) may include wreck diving with no penetration, d) may involve waves or some current, e) may involve open water sites with boat entries, f) has good to moderate visibility, and g) may have other conditions which may warrant more experience.

An advanced dive: a) may reach depths between 100' and 130', b) is suitable for very experienced divers (may prefer specialty certification), c) may involve limited wreck penetration, swift or variable current diving, cold water, or ice diving, d) may have extremely limited or zero visibility, e) may require special skills such as navigation, rescue, cave or cavern diving training or special equipment.

Regarding safety during scuba diving: use common sense and neither neglect nor forget nor ignore your training and your limitations.

- DIVING HAZARDS: These are given in very general terms and are extremely variable and weather-dependent. Make personal on-site evaluations before you scuba dive in unfamiliar waters.

- CO-ORDINATES: These are the exact locations of each shipwreck, given in either latitude/longitude (GPS, Global Positioning System), or TD's (time differentials) for the older Loran system, or both, if known. Unfortunately, there are variations between even the same brand of electronics, so proceed doing a search pattern with a depth sounder and patience if you don't locate the shipwreck immediately.

Finally, the author is well aware that compiling a list of "the 100 best" Great Lakes shipwrecks is inviting controversy and debate. However, he does not feel like changing his lifestyle now. The author is also aware that "the 100 best" list will change with future shipwreck discoveries, and these newly-discovered shipwrecks will have the diver education and protective legislation introduced all around the Great Lakes in recent years to protect and conserve their intact states.

These two books about "The 100 Best Great Lakes Shipwrecks" are meant to provide the reader with exciting tales of maritime history, and, for the scuba diver, reveal and describe shipwrecks that are the most interesting in the world to explore.

Have fun!

Cris Kohl
High Lake, Illinois,
August, 1998

4 Lake Michigan Shipwrecks

THE FIRST DRAW-BRIDGE IN CHICAGO.

The most recent glacial period, or Ice Age, which consisted of four stages combining to last over a million years, ended only about 12,000 years ago. Initial drainage flowed south into the Mississippi River, a situation which ended only about 4,000-5,000 years ago when the "Chicago outlet" on Lake Michigan closed, and all of the Great Lakes drained exclusively into the St. Lawrence River.

The year was 1634 when the French explorer, Jean Nicolet, canoed into Lake Michigan's north shore and Green Bay area, becoming the first European to see these waters. The lake was at first illogically referred to as the "Lake of Stinking Water," seemingly because the Native American group that resided here had migrated from the "paunt," or "stinking" (salt) water, possibly Hudson Bay, years earlier. The lake as we know it today was named after the Algonquian term, "Michigami," meaning "large body of water."

Here are some quick facts about the lake:

- Lake Michigan is bordered by Michigan on the north and east, Wisconsin on the west, Illinois on the southwest, and Indiana on the southeast.

- Lake Michigan, the third largest of the Great Lakes, is 321 miles long and 118 miles wide at its greatest points. This is the only one of the five Great Lakes which surrounds all 22,300 square miles of its surface area entirely within the boundaries of the United States.

- The deepest part of Lake Michigan descends to an overwhelming 923 feet, or about 154 fathoms, at a point about 26 miles WSW of Point Betsey Light, and about 33 miles ESE from the Sturgeon Bay Ship Canal Light. The average, or mean depth, of Lake Michigan is 276 feet.

- Approximately 100 rivers of varying sizes maintain the water level in Lake Michigan. Slight currents flow counterclockwise in the lake, drifting south along the west side and north along the east. Although Lake Michigan flows into Lake Huron at the Straits of Mackinac, scientists have conjectured that the retention time of water in Lake Michigan is almost 100 years!

- The largest city on Lake Michigan is Chicago, a community which grew in leaps and bounds initially jump-started by saturation shipping. The small community of Chicago had regular passenger ship service in 1830 when it was founded. The first steam locomotive arrived for use in Chicago on board a sailing ship in 1837. The population of Chicago was only 30,000 in 1850; by 1900, this had leaped to 1,700,000, and it more than doubled by 1950 to 3,600,000! Chicago's early importance as a Great Lakes port can be seen in this news item from the *Cleveland Herald* of December 6, 1882: "Chicago has entered a solemn protest against the hackneyed assertion that the most important ports in the world are respectively Liverpool, London, Glasgow, and New York, and makes good her claim that her tonnage is greater than the first three combined, taking the year 1878 as the test season. The figures as given stand as follows: Liverpool, 2,647,372; London, 2,330,688; Glasgow, 1,432,264; New York, 1,153,676; giving a total of 7,564,000. This, it is claimed, is only 324,327 tons more than Chicago's record, which for the above year was 7,239,678."

- The first actual ship to visit Lake Michigan was LaSalle's famed *Griffon* in 1679. It loaded up with furs at Green Bay and headed back towards Niagara at eastern Lake Erie, but disappeared on this maiden voyage with all hands, probably at the western end of Manitoulin Island in Lake Huron (see the Lake Huron description).

- The first shipwreck on Lake Michigan was the schooner, *Hercules,* wrecked in 1818 with all hands off what is now Chicago's 63rd Street. By the time a Native American group found the human remains along the shoreline a few days later, wolves and bears had mutilated the bodies beyond recognition. The challenges facing the Lake Michigan pioneers are unimaginable today.

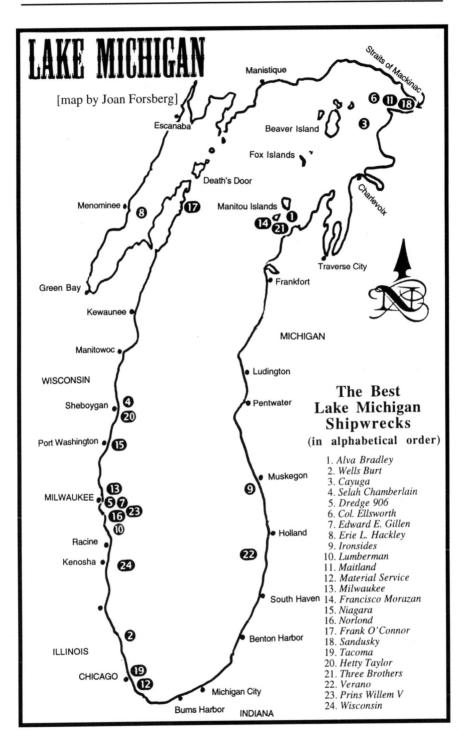

LAKE MICHIGAN

[map by Joan Forsberg]

Straits of Mackinac

Manistique

6 11 18

Beaver Island

3

Escanaba

Fox Islands

Death's Door

Charlevoix

Menominee • 8 17

Manitou Islands

14 1
21

Green Bay

Traverse City

Kewaunee •

Frankfort

Manitowoc •

MICHIGAN

WISCONSIN

Ludington

Sheboygan • 4
20

Pentwater

Port Washington • 15

**The Best
Lake Michigan
Shipwrecks**

(in alphabetical order)

1. *Alva Bradley*
2. *Wells Burt*
3. *Cayuga*
4. *Selah Chamberlain*
5. *Dredge 906*
6. *Col. Ellsworth*
7. *Edward E. Gillen*
8. *Erie L. Hackley*
9. *Ironsides*
10. *Lumberman*
11. *Maitland*
12. *Material Service*
13. *Milwaukee*
14. *Francisco Morazan*
15. *Niagara*
16. *Norlond*
17. *Frank O'Connor*
18. *Sandusky*
19. *Tacoma*
20. *Hetty Taylor*
21. *Three Brothers*
22. *Verano*
23. *Prins Willem V*
24. *Wisconsin*

Muskegon

13 9
MILWAUKEE • 5 7
16 23
10

Holland

Racine

22

Kenosha • 24

South Haven

2

Benton Barbor

ILLINOIS

19
CHICAGO • 12

Michigan City

Burns Harbor   INDIANA

- The 265-foot-long, five-masted schooner, *David Dows,* the largest sailing vessel ever constructed on the Great Lakes (this was at Toledo, Ohio, in 1881), ended its career in 40 feet of Lake Michigan water just off Chicago in a fierce gale which broke the ship's spine on November 25, 1889.

- Lake Michigan has sadly played host to the all-time worst maritime disaster on the Great Lakes when the passenger steamer, *Eastland,* tipped over at its dock in Chicago on July 24, 1915, with over 2,500 excursionists on board ready to depart for a day of fun. Approximately 835 of them drowned. The ship was righted and returned to service, but business waned, so the *Eastland* became the *Wilmette,* a naval training vessel. She definitely carried many nervous sailors in those years before she was finally scrapped.

- Lake Michigan has had more than its fair shore of tragic ship losses, including the sinking of the steamer, *Lady Elgin,* after a collision with the schooner, *Augusta,* on the night of September 8, 1860, off Winnetka, Illinois; about 300 people lost their lives. The steamer, *Seabird,* caught on fire off Waukegan, Illinois, on April 9, 1868; there were only two survivors from the total of over 100 on board. The steamer, *Phoenix,* on her final run of the season, caught on fire near Sheboygan, Wisconsin, on the night of November 21, 1847, while carrying about 250 Dutch settlers to the western frontier; about 200 men, women, and children died in this catastrophe. The steamer, *Alpena,* went missing in a storm somewhere off Holland, Michigan, on October 15, 1880, with the loss of everyone on board, about 80 people. Both the *Lady Elgin* and the *Seabird* were located by Chicago diver Harry Zych in the 1980's; the court battles for salvage rights continue.

- In 1867, a Capt. McBride, who had crossed Lake Michigan "times into the thousands," reported that the lake was "inhabited by something bigger and of a more amphibious nature than the whitefish or the sturgeon...." He claimed to have seen a freshwater whale. Another captain reported seeing "a monster...which looked big enough to destroy a boat at one blow.... Its head is large and its jaws capacious...." *(Toledo Blade,* August 1, 1867). So-called sea monsters have been reportedly seen in every one of the Great Lakes, but their existence is likely attributable to sailors' over-indulgence in boredom, imagination, and/or rum.

- The Treaty of 1872 gave Canadian and British ships the right to navigate Lake Michigan; in turn, U.S. vessels have the right to navigate the St. Lawrence River.

- There are approximately 950 shipwrecks in Lake Michigan.

- One of Michigan's nine Bottomland Preserves is on Lake Michigan at Manitou Passage near Traverse City, and a proposed preserve in the state's southwest corner in the Holland/South Haven area could become a definite entity soon.

Bradley, Alva (#1 on the map on p. 269)

VESSEL NAME:	ALVA BRADLEY
RIG:	three-masted schooner
DIMENSIONS:	192' 2" x 32' x 20' 2"
LAUNCHED:	1870; Cleveland, Ohio
DATE LOST:	Saturday, October 13, 1894
CAUSE OF LOSS:	foundered during a gale
CARGO:	steel billets
LIVES LOST:	none
GENERAL LOCATION:	SE of North Manitou Island, Michigan
DEPTH:	20' - 27'
ACCESS:	boat
DIVING SKILL LEVEL:	novice
DIVING HAZARDS:	minimal
CO-ORDINATES:	Lat/Lon: 45.02.27 / 85.59.26
	Loran: 31798.5 / 48339.2

Veteran Great Lakes shipwreck sleuth, David Trotter, who lives in the Detroit area, was running his boat and sidescan sonar unit through the dangerous waters of Manitou Passage in Lake Michigan in the spring of 1990 when, in about 30' of water, he got a hit on the printout. He had been searching for the lost-with-all-hands steamer, *W.H. Gilcher,* but instead found the well-preserved remains of the three-masted schooner, *Alva Bradley.*

The discovery of the *Alva Bradley* rekindled excitement in Michigan's Manitou Passage Underwater Preserve.

Some words on the underwater parks/preserves systems are in order here. Michigan followed Ontario's lead in recognizing certain areas as requiring special status due to their high concentrations of shipwrecks. The first Great Lakes underwater park was created at Tobermory, Ontario, in 1972. The first Michigan Underwater Preserve was designated in 1980. An underwater park involves government spending; an underwater preserve does not. Fathom Five National Underwater Park began as a province of Ontario park, with limited provincial funding; when it went federal in 1987, it received increased (federal) funding to maintain and expand the park office, personnel, buoy markers, and policing. Management of underwater preserves in Michigan is in the hands of local preserve support groups (volunteers) and a Michigan Underwater Preserves

Council, with the state contributing little or no funds towards showcasing or maintaining the preserves. Other U.S. states are eyeing Michigan's system.

Michigan's nine areas where underwater preserves have been created are at Alger County (the Munising area, on Lake Superior), Thunder Bay (the Alpena area on Lake Huron), the Straits of Mackinac (where Lakes Michigan and Huron meet), Whitefish Point (on Lake Superior), Marquette County (off Marquette, Michigan, on Lake Superior), the Keweenaw Peninsula area (on Lake Superior), the Thumb Area (off Pointe aux Barques on Lake Huron), Sanilac Shores off Port Sanilac (in lower Lake Huron), and Manitou Passage (in Lake Michigan); two more have been proposed, one in Southwest Michigan (in Lake Michigan) and another in the DeTour Passage area (in upper Lake Huron).

But let us return to the story of the schooner, *Alva Bradley*.

The three-masted, steel-rigged, 192-foot, wooden schooner, ALVA BRADLEY, *was launched at Cleveland in 1870 and sank in about 30' of water on October 13, 1894, at North Manitou Island in Lake Michigan.* GREAT LAKES MARINE COLLECTION OF THE MILWAUKEE PUBLIC LIBRARY/WISCONSIN MARINE HISTORICAL SOCIETY.

The bow section of the schooner, *Alva Bradley*

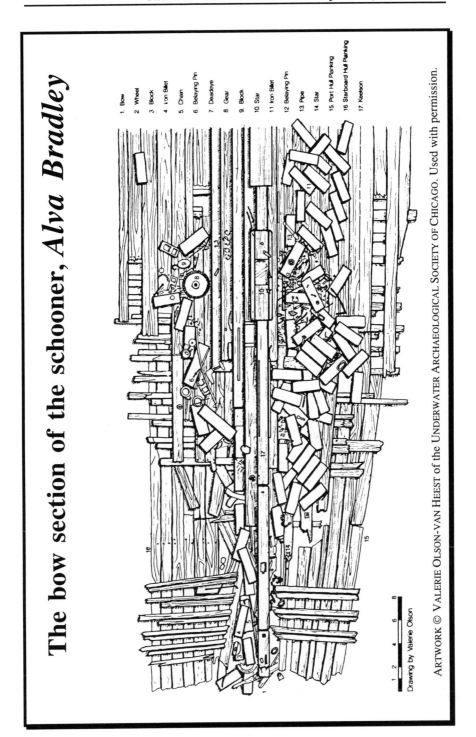

1. Bow
2. Wheel
3. Block
4. Iron Billet
5. Chain
6. Belaying Pin
7. Deadeye
8. Gear
9. Block
10. Star
11. Iron Billet
12. Belaying Pin
13. Pipe
14. Star
15. Port Hull Planking
16. Starboard Hull Planking
17. Keelson

Drawing by Valerie Olson

ARTWORK © VALERIE OLSON-VAN HEEST of the UNDERWATER ARCHAEOLOGICAL SOCIETY OF CHICAGO. Used with permission.

On Saturday, October 13, 1894, the *Alva Bradley,* loaded with steel billets from Fairport, Ohio, bound for Milwaukee, sprang a leak during a severe gale while 20 miles off North Manitou Island. The ship was towed by the steamer, *Jay S. Fay,* along with another towed vessel, the schooner, *S.H. Kimball,* all of them belonging to the Bradley fleet of Cleveland. Captain Peterson of the *Bradley* immediately headed his damaged vessel to the lee of the island, where his ship sank. The crew of six men and one woman, in response to their distress signals, were rescued by the U.S. Life Saving Service crew, seven miles southwest of their station on North Manitou Island. The *Bradley* crew was later placed on board the steamer, *Douglas,* and conveyed to Traverse City on the Michigan mainland. The uninsured *Alva Bradley* was valued at $20,000, with her cargo, which had been insured for 80% of its value, worth $25,000.

Initial newspaper reports indicated that the *Alva Bradley,* which lay in "about five fathoms [30'] of water, with four feet of water over the rail at amidships," could possibly be salvaged. The vessel was not in deep water, and her owners had had the ship thoroughly recaulked the previous summer during a stretch of nautical inactivity. The ship, although 24 years old, was reportedly "in good condition." The wrecking vessel, *Favorite,* took lumber to the *Bradley* wreck site in hopes of nailing shut any obvious damage and pumping the vessel dry. But the weather stayed very unpleasant for wrecking, and when the *Favorite* reached the site, the *Alva Bradley* was broken up except for about 50' of her bow, which still carried an upright foremast. Captain Harris Baker, with the steamer, *Snook,* undertook the recovery and salvage of the cargo of steel billets from the *Alva Bradley,* claiming 40% of their value as his compensation. He was not able to salvage the entire cargo, as some of the billets remain at the site.

The *Alva Bradley's* last document of registration was surrendered at Cleveland on April 27, 1895, giving the reason as "vessel lost."

The 934-gross-ton, steel-rigged *Alva Bradley,* built by Quayle & Martin of Cleveland, Ohio, in 1870, measured 192' 2" in length, 32' in beam, and 20' 2" in draft (these were not the ship's original tonnage and measurements, but her final ones based on a rebuild in 1888). The vessel, owned her entire life by the Bradleys of Cleveland, was first enrolled with official number 1910 on July 6, 1870. The *Alva Bradley* experienced a serious grounding (and a dramatic rescue of her crew) on October 24, 1887, at Shot Point, near Marquette on Lake Superior. The ship was recovered ten days later and returned to service.

The wreck offers many artifact sights: divers initially located a pipe, eyeglasses, a leather purse containing old coins, a toilet, and a stove; today's visitors can appreciate the ship's wheel, blocks, chains, deadeyes, belaying pins, keelson, many tools, some machinery, and a large portion of the cargo of steel billets. Try to catch the shipwreck displays in Glen Haven, Michigan, at the Sleeping Bear Point Coast Guard Station Maritime Museum.

Burt, Wells
(#2 on the map on p. 269)

VESSEL NAME:	WELLS BURT
RIG:	three-masted schooner
DIMENSIONS:	201' x 33' 5" x 14' 2"
LAUNCHED:	Saturday, July 12, 1873; Detroit, Michigan
DATE LOST:	Sunday, May 20, 1883
CAUSE OF LOSS:	foundered in a storm
CARGO:	coal
LIVES LOST:	all hands (11)
GENERAL LOCATION:	off Evanston, Illinois
DEPTH:	38' - 45'
ACCESS:	boat
DIVING SKILL LEVEL:	novice-intermediate
DIVING HAZARDS:	minimal: silting
CO-ORDINATES:	Lat/Lon: 42.02.52 / 87.37.56
	Loran: 33325.5 / 49977.8

The short, ten-year life of the three-masted schooner, *Wells Burt,* spanned five owners: H. Coyne and Geo. Allen of Detroit (1873-1876), J. Allen of Detroit (1876-1878), E. Stone of Milwaukee (1878-1880), L. Kelly of Milwaukee (1880-1883), and J.S. Dunham of Chicago (1883).

Measuring 201' in length, 33' 5" in beam, and 14' 2" in draft, the 756-gross-ton schooner, *Wells Burt* (official number 80365), slid solidly down the launchramp of the Detroit Dry Dock Company on July 12, 1873, "a staunchly built vessel," as the press reported. The *Wells Burt* was considered a first-class schooner engaged mostly in the iron ore, coal, and grain trade.

As staunchly built as she was, the *Wells Burt* could not withstand the storm which covered most of Lake Michigan on May 20, 1883. The *Burt,* loaded with 1,540 tons of anthracite coal, enroute from Buffalo to Chicago, almost made it to her destination. This was the return leg of her first trip of the season, having left Chicago at the opening of navigation on May 1st with 53,000 bushels of corn for Buffalo. Unfortunately the waves were now so high and the winds were so powerful that over three dozen ships were at anchor outside Chicago harbor trying to ride out the storm before attempting an entry into that narrow refuge. The *Wells Burt* was on her way home to Chicago when she sailed into the eye of that storm.

The schooner, *Wells Burt*

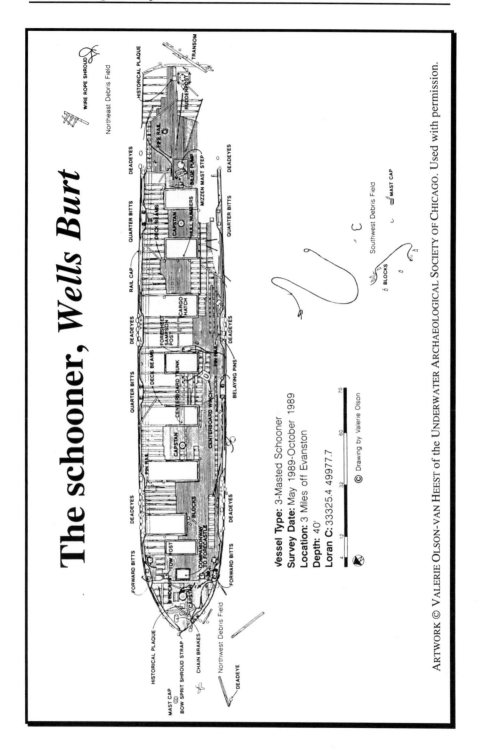

Vessel Type: 3-Masted Schooner
Survey Date: May 1989-October 1989
Location: 3 Miles off Evanston
Depth: 40'
Loran C: 33325.4 49977.7

© Drawing by Valerie Olson

ARTWORK © VALERIE OLSON-VAN HEEST of the UNDERWATER ARCHAEOLOGICAL SOCIETY OF CHICAGO. Used with permission.

The schooner, *Wells Burt*

ARTWORK © VALERIE OLSON-VAN HEEST of the UNDERWATER ARCHAEOLOGICAL SOCIETY OF CHICAGO. Used with permission.

When the sun rose the next day, the *Wells Burt* was nowhere in sight. Her deckhouse was discovered on the beach near the waterworks by a policeman. More flotsam from the *Burt* was steadily washing ashore. The upper rigging of a sunken schooner stuck out from the offshore waters and was identified by owner Dunham as being that of the *Wells Burt,* sitting in 40' of water. She had been sailed by Captain Thomas Fountain, "one of the most experienced and capable men on the lakes." Also on board were his son, Dan, first mate William F. "Pensaukee Bill" Cody, and eight others. All were lost. The *Wells Burt,* valued at $30,000, was insured for $25,700; she had cost $40,000 to build ten years earlier. The coal cargo was insured for its full value of $7,500. Speculation was that another ship had collided with the *Burt;* hardhat diver Peter Falcon, who salvaged the anchors, felt that a broken rudder had caused the ship to founder.

Drawing of the 192' schooner, WELLS BURT. GREAT LAKES MARINE COLLECTION OF THE MILWAUKEE PUBLIC LIBRARY/WISCONSIN MARINE HISTORICAL SOCIETY.

Located in 1988 by professional divers from A&T Recovery of Chicago, the wreck of the *Wells Burt* was surveyed and photographed extensively in 1989 by divers from the Underwater Archaeological Society of Chicago. Maintaining the integrity of the shipwreck succeeded for a while. In May, 1991, however, a diver stole ten deadeyes from the site. As a result, UASC divers, under state permit, removed a number of loose artifacts which were conserved at the Chicago Maritime Museum, and chained the remaining deadeyes to the hull. A reward of $2,000 was offered for information leading to the arrest and conviction of the thief. Contact the Illinois Historic Preservation Agency or the State Police. Hopefully the *Wells Burt* will not be stripped to the bone as have so many other non-renewable Great Lakes shipwrecks.

Cayuga

(#3 on the map on p. 269)

VESSEL NAME:	CAYUGA
RIG:	steel propeller
DIMENSIONS:	290' x 40' 8" x 13' 6"
LAUNCHED:	Tuesday, April 2, 1889; Cleveland, Ohio
DATE LOST:	Friday, May 10, 1895
CAUSE OF LOSS:	collision with the steamer, JOSEPH L. HURD
CARGO:	package freight
LIVES LOST:	none (1 life lost from the JOSEPH L. HURD)
GENERAL LOCATION:	near Skillagalee Light, SW of Mackinac
DEPTH:	75' - 102'
ACCESS:	boat
DIVING SKILL LEVEL:	advanced
DIVING HAZARDS:	depth, penetration, silting, hypothermia
CO-ORDINATES:	Lat/Lon: 45.43.19 / 85.11.36
	Loran: 31390.4 / 48089.8

It was like a major stock market collapse for Great Lakes insurance underwriters when an old steamer valued at a mere $15,000 collided with and sank a modern, fully insured freighter worth $175,000 carrying a cargo of flour, oats, and general merchandise worth a total of $90,000, also fully insured.

The two ships unwillingly steamed towards each other in a dense fog combined with 4:00 A.M. darkness on the morning of Friday, May 10, 1895. The 26-year-old *Joseph L. Hurd*, of the Lake Michigan & Lake Superior Transportation Company, was bound from Duluth to Chicago with a load of lumber on deck and package freight below. The six-year-old *Cayuga,* of the Lehigh Valley Steamship Company, had left Chicago heading for Buffalo with a load of flour and general merchandise.

The wind blew deceptively across the ships' beams, distorting any sounds such as fog whistles which were being emitted. The two vessels neared each other just south of Skilligalee Light off Charlevoix in northern Lake Michigan, not too many miles southwest of the Straits of Mackinac. They had seen each other's lights when they were about ten miles apart, but a thick fogbank moved in and hid the ships from each other.

Both steamers were only a few hundred feet apart when their signals were distinguished. The *Cayuga* quickly slammed her engine into reverse, which slowed the ship down considerably, but it was too late to avoid a collision. The 290-foot, 2,669-gross-ton steel youngster, *Cayuga,* and the 171-foot, 592-gross-ton wooden senior, *Joseph L. Hurd,* collided violently. It should have been no contest, but surprisingly, it was the *Cayuga* that sank!

One *Cayuga* sailor later described the collision: "It was an awful shock. It knocked every man out of his bunk, and they came up in all sorts of dress, running around the deck in a terrified state, shouting and yelling and crying for help...."

Painting of the steamer, CAYUGA, *by Rev. Edward J. Dowling, S.J., done in 1950 based on his historical research.* GREAT LAKES MARINE COLLECTION OF THE MILWAUKEE PUBLIC LIBRARY/WISCONSIN MARINE HISTORICAL SOCIETY.

The smaller, older, wooden steamer struck the newer, steel ship abreast of the *Cayuga's* forward hatch on the starboard side, tearing a hole six feet deep and two feet wide into the metal hull. The *Cayuga's* speed at the time of impact completely and deftly sheered off the *Hurd's* entire forward section. The sailors on the *Hurd,* taking stock of their situation after the initial shock of the collision wore off, could not believe their eyes. They were on board a ship which no longer had a bow! The *Hurd's* load of lumber, however, kept the steamer afloat.

ABOVE: *Captain James Reid used the tugboat,* PROTECTOR, *and eight huge air-filled steel pontoons (two of which are pictured here) which he planned to attach to the wreck of the* CAYUGA *in his unsuccessful attempts to raise the steamer.* AUTHOR'S COLLECTION.   BELOW: *Diver Frank Troxell heads past a portion of steel railing along the angled deck of the* CAYUGA, *which sits in 102' of water.*   PHOTO BY CRIS KOHL.

The situation was worse on board the *Cayuga,* where a large part of the hole in her side was below the waterline. With her heavier displacement and heftier cargo, the *Cayuga* was clearly on her way to the bottom. Her crew took to the lifeboats. Only 25 minutes after the collision, the *Cayuga* sank in an estimated 15 fathoms of water. The crews of both ships remained at the scene for about an hour when the passing steamer, *Manola* (see *The 100 Best Great Lakes Shipwrecks, Volume I,* pp. 19-22), picked them up. The *Cayuga* sank, but the only human casualty was from the *Hurd* when the old bachelor/steward/cook, George Johnson, was knocked overboard and drowned. The *Joseph L. Hurd* was towed to Harbor Springs the day after the collision by the wrecking tug, *Favorite,* and repaired. The *Hurd,* belonged to an earlier class of steamships, being constructed from wood and fitted with huge, wooden arches to strengthen the hull. For years, she carried passengers, but was reduced to a lumber carrier in 1892. The *Hurd,* valued at $15,000, was insured for $10,800.

On the day after the collision, the Chicago press made it clear that any salvage would be difficult. "...Among practical marine men, it was believed that the steamer *[Cayuga]* could ultimately be got afloat again, but it was thought the expense would amount to nearly all she was worth. The work must be done with pontoons and will be a long, tedious job at best...." It had cost $250,000 to build the *Cayuga* in 1889.

Four days after the sinking, a jingoistic newspaper report stated that "The lake underwriters are shedding no tears over the disaster [because] the bulk of the loss is held by the British & Foreign and other 'blawsted' English companies, and the loss to the lake men is trifling...."

Five days after the *Cayuga* sank, wrecking master Sinclair of Chicago, returned from a day of searching for the wreck site, stated that the vessel must lie in 102 to 120 feet of water, and he expressed his doubts that it could ever be raised. The wreck was found shortly thereafter, but now a salvager was needed!

On September 5, 1895, Captain James Reid and Sons of Bay City, Michigan, signed a contract with the underwriters to raise the steamer, *Cayuga,* for a fee of $100,000. This 290-foot, 2,669-gross-ton steamer was heavier than any ship which had ever been salvaged before from such a depth (a bit more than 100'), and no cranes or other lifting equipment existed to raise such a load. Captain Reid, pressured to uphold an enormous reputation for successful salvaging, stubbornly spent thousands of dollars (to the point where he temporarily crippled his company) and four years of time in his relentless pursuit for success in raising the *Cayuga.* In the end, he failed to attain his goal.

Reid decided on the previously recommended course of salvage; he would sink eight enormous steel pontoons, lash them to the sides of the steamer with thick cables, pump air into them, lift the *Cayuga* somewhat off the lake bottom with the help of a barge, and tow the wreck gradually into shallow water where it could be repaired. Reid and several of his divers suffered serious injuries such as the "bends," and at least one hardhat diver lost his life here.

The steamer, *Cayuga*

ARTWORK © CHUCK AND JERI FELTNER. Used with permission.

Great Lakes lore has it that one of Reid's hardhat divers died when he was trapped beneath the salvage barge when it sank next to the *Cayuga,* and that his severed air hose was sticking out from that barge when Illinois shipwreck hunters John Steele and Gene Turner located the wreck of the *Cayuga* in the spring of 1969. The salvage barge is definitely (and the hardhat diver is reputedly) still there.

By late 1898, after more than three expensive years of trying to raise the *Cayuga,* James Reid had changed his manner. The DETROIT FREE PRESS of November 9, 1898, revealed, "The quiet weather season has again come and gone, and still the *Cayuga* lies at the bottom of Lake Michigan. Passing vessels report that lighters, etc., have been hovering around the scene of the neighborhood of the spot where she lies, and that a heavy-set, active figure, strongly resembling that of Capt. James Reid, has been sighted directing operations. But that is the extent of the knowledge the public has of the big task this year. Reid has been so bothered by publicity about his operations that he is keeping a very close mouth. It is not known now whether he is sanguine of success, or fearful of failure. In years gone by it was all hope with him." Contrary to his reputation and personality, James Reid gave up on raising the *Cayuga* not too long after this.

The *Cayuga* was one of five expensive, steel ships, all of the same design, built for the Lehigh Valley Transportation Company by the Globe Iron Works Company of Cleveland, Ohio, in 1888-1890: the *E.P. Wilbur, Cayuga, Seneca, Saranac,* and *Tuscarora.* These fast ships carried package freight between Buffalo, Chicago, and Milwaukee.

The *Cayuga's* hull was almost completely stripped by salvager James Reid in the late 1890's. It lies on a 35-degree angle to portside. The gash from the collision on the starboard side of the bow is quite evident. The double-decked hull is easily penetrated (but training, experience, and preparation are necessary), providing interesting views of the triple expansion engine and boiler. The huge, four-bladed propeller is still in place, with a spare propeller blade below deck in the hatch closest to the stern.

About 40' off the port side lies a 75-foot-long workbarge used in the unsuccessful salvage attempt, supposedly sunk when an air-filled steel pontoon suddenly broke loose from the *Cayuga* and shot to the surface. According to the story, this barge sank right on top of one of Reid's hardhat divers. Several steel pontoons are still strapped in place along both sides of the ship's stern as a reminder to visiting divers that perhaps the greatest of all Great Lakes commercial salvagers failed to raise the *Cayuga* over a hundred years ago.

Chamberlain, Selah

(#4 on the map on p. 269)

VESSEL NAME:	SELAH CHAMBERLAIN
RIG:	wooden steam barge
DIMENSIONS:	212' x 34' x 14'
LAUNCHED:	1873; Cleveland, Ohio
DATE LOST:	Wednesday, October 13, 1886
CAUSE OF LOSS:	collision with steamer, JOHN PRIDGEON, JR.
CARGO:	none
LIVES LOST:	5 (from 16 on board)
GENERAL LOCATION:	2 miles NE of Sheboygan Point, Wisconsin
DEPTH:	75' - 88'
ACCESS:	boat
DIVING SKILL LEVEL:	advanced
DIVING HAZARDS:	depth, silting, disorientation, hypothermia
CO-ORDINATES:	Lat/Lon: 43.46.12 / 87.34.47
	Loran: 32670.7 / 48828.0

The 1,207-gross-ton *Selah Chamberlain,* a wooden steam barge sitting in about 90' of water, is one of Wisconsin's most popular dive sites.

Why? The wreck rests in an area of reliably good visibility. There is much to see, e.g. the boilers and machinery are upright and intact, with gears, piston, drive shaft, and propeller in place; tools from the ship abound at this site. Local scuba dive shops usually buoy this shipwreck. Lastly, dive shops, charter boats, and boat launching facilities are located in nearby Sheboygan.

Often the shifting sands at the shipwreck site will cover and uncover portions of the wreck, making it look different each time you explore it!

The 1,207-gross-ton *Selah Chamberlain* was a course freight steamer which carried primarily iron ore, grain, and coal cargoes. Later she also towed schooner-barges carrying the same loads. Built by Quayle & Martin for Alva Bradley at Cleveland, Ohio, in 1873, the *Chamberlain* (official number 115147) measured 212' in length, 34' in beam, and 14' in draft. In 1875, two years after she was built, the vessel was valued at $65,000. She was rebuilt in 1883. By 1885, her value had dropped to only $55,000. The rebuild helped, but even so, the *Chamberlain* was considered a stout, well-maintained ship.

Unfortunately, on Wed., October 13, 1886, the steamer, *Selah Chamberlain*, bound light from Milwaukee to Escanaba, Michigan, to pick up a load of iron ore, sank after a collision with the 221', 1,212-gross-ton steamer, *John Pridgeon, Jr.,* bound from Odgensburg to Chicago with general merchandise, in dense fog off Sheboygan. Five lives were needlessly lost in a careless accident.

The Marine Record reported this story, dated October 14, 1886:

"The steamer *Selah Chamberlain* left Milwaukee light at 3:30 yesterday afternoon, bound for Escanaba. The weather was thick, with the wind blowing a stiff breeze from the south. The steamer was sounding her whistle at regular intervals. At 8:30, when off Sheboygan harbor, and about seven miles out in the lake, they heard another steamer whistle directly ahead and close aboard. The captain of the *Chamberlain* sounded one blast from his whistle and put his wheel aport, when, without any other warning, the two steamers came together. The wind and sea immediately separated them. The *Chamberlain* kept sounding her whistle for assistance, but no assistance coming, the crew proceeded to launch their lifeboat. When they got their smallest lifeboat swung over the side, and ready to lower into the water, seven of the crew ran and jumped into the boat, and their combined weights broke the davits, and five of them fell into the water. Two men, the cook and steward, being under the thwarts of the boat, were not thrown out, but the other five were not seen again.

"The crew of the *Chamberlain* then got their largest lifeboat into the water; the rest of the men got into her, picked up the small lifeboat, and transferred part of the crew into her. Just as they got clear of the steamer, she sunk to her mastheads. The smallest of the lifeboats went back and got the steamer's stern light, which was above water, put the light into the large lifeboat so that they could see the compass to steer by, and then in tow of the large boat they pulled for the shore, where they arrived at 1:15....The *Chamberlain* was struck on the port bow and was cut down to below the water line...."

Thus one generation's tragedy provided a later generation's recreation.

STRUCK ON THE PORT BOW.

The Steam Barge Selah Chamberlain Sunk by the John Pridgeon, Jr.

THE COLLISION OCCURS IN A DENSE FOG AND HEAVY GALE.

Five Lives Lost—The Second Engineer, Fireman and Three Deck Hands.

Headlines in the DETROIT FREE PRESS, *Oct. 15, 1886, about the* SELAH CHAMBERLAIN.

Dredge 906 (#5 on the map on p. 269)

VESSEL NAME:	Dredge 906
RIG:	dredge
DIMENSIONS:	110' x 40'
LAUNCHED:	1912
DATE LOST:	Wednesday, May 23, 1956
CAUSE OF LOSS:	capsized
CARGO:	none
LIVES LOST:	9 (from crew of 19)
GENERAL LOCATION:	several miles off Milwaukee, Wisconsin
DEPTH:	30' - 55'
ACCESS:	boat
DIVING SKILL LEVEL:	intermediate
DIVING HAZARDS:	penetration, silting, hypothermia
CO-ORDINATES:	Lat/Lon: 42.57.92 / 87.47.24
	Loran: 32996.0 / 49329.1

The modern, tragic sinking of *Dredge 906*, a steel-hulled, box-type, nonself-propelled, uninspected, unregistered "vessel" just off Milwaukee on Wednesday, May 23, 1956, with the loss of nine lives, was labeled "The Worst Toll in Years!" by one Milwaukee newspaper.

The 685-(approximately)-gross-ton dredge, built at Manitowoc, Wisconsin, in 1912, measured 110' in length, 40' in beam, and 11' 5" in draft. It was fitted with a boom and a dipper, with necessary power, as well as auxiliary machinery and equipment for dredging purposes. It had been engaged in dredging operations about 11 miles south of Milwaukee in Lake Michigan off Oak Creek, Wisconsin, dredging the turning basin at the Wisconsin Electric Power Plant. The dredge carried a wooden housing, or superstructure, which protected certain machinery and equipment and provided accommodations and galley facilities for the workers employed by the dredging company.

This housing was not constructed to withstand rough weather on the open lake. It was intended for harbor, or some other safe refuge, work.

On Tuesday evening, May 22, 1956, the wind began to pick up. A storm was on its way. At 10:50 P.M., because of the worsening weather conditions, it was decided that discretion was the better part of valor, and that this dredge was not constructed for rough waters. However, instead of removing the crew as quickly as possible while leaving the dredge out there, or instead of towing the dredge with its crew to nearby Oak Creek, the decision was made by the dredge's night master, Captain Martin E. Walsh, to tow the dredge with its crew all the way to Milwaukee harbor. The 95-gross-ton, 78-foot tug, *E. James Fucik*, began towing.

The dredge was towed stern first, meaning that the dipper end, normally at the "bow", became the "stern" during towing. A one and one-eighth inch towing cable with a scope of 900' was attached to both sides of the dredge's second timberhead. At 11:00 P.M., second in command, operator Edwin Selvick, ordered the dredge crew to don lifejackets. Captain Walsh was standing by at the shovel controls in the lever house.

The 110' steel-hulled DREDGE 906, *built in 1912, sank with the loss of nine lives off Milwaukee on May 23, 1956. It sits upside-down in 55'.*   AUTHOR'S COLLECTION.

The weather worsened and *Dredge 906* started taking on water, particularly from the leaky superstructure that the 19 men on board called their floating home. The dredge was a vessel consisting of a steel hull, a steel main deck, and wooden deckhousing. There were four athwartship compartments, separated by nonwatertight bulkheads. Suddenly *Dredge 906* leaned to one side on a starboard list, and a guy wire holding the dipper boom in place parted. Captain Walsh blew the danger signal of five or more blasts on his whistle, but the tug crew did not hear it. The boom swung to the starboard and the list increased.

Two barrels rolled against the lever house, trapping 62-year-old Captain Walsh inside the structure. Selvick helped the captain crawl out through one of the windows. By now, the deck was leaning at an angle of about 45 degrees, and most of the men were gathered on the high portside.

Selvick shouted, "Jump." Nobody moved. Noticing their obvious reluctance, Selvick jumped first and then the rest followed. All were wearing lifejackets. About 45 seconds later, *Dredge 906* capsized and sank.

It was 2:15 A.M., Wednesday, May 23, 1956. *Dredge 906* was approximately 2.5 miles off shore and about 6.5 miles from the Milwaukee Breakwater Light. Water temperature was between 45 and 50 degrees.

So sudden was the capsize that there had been no time to launch the dredge's wooden, 16' yawl boat. All persons on board, with the possible exception of one or two who were trapped inside the superstructure, were on deck and wearing lifejackets at the time of sinking.

Worst Lake Toll in Years!
Waves Capsize Dredge, 9 Drown

10 Rescued In Icy Water Off Cudahy

An air and sea search continued Wednesday for the bodies of two of nine men who drowned off Cudahy earlier in the day in one of Lake Michigan's worst tragedies of recent years.

(The drowning of the nine men was the second tragedy within 12 hours in that area of the lake

swinging wildly in the storm, the dredge capsized within a minute dumping all aboard into the cold lake.

Three bodies were recovered by the Fucik shortly after the accident, and four others were picked up later by the Coast Guard.

All ten men rescued were hospitalized and seven remained in Johnston Municipal Hospital Wednesday night suffering from exposure and bruises.

WORKED ROUND CLOCK

The 120 by 40 foot dredge had been operating round the clock at the new Oak Creek power plant of the Electric Co. dredging a channel for coal boats to the plant.

When the storm struck from out of the north Tuesday night,

Sturgeon Bay, who roomed at 620 N. 10th St.; Arne O. Wold, 57, Chicago; Joseph Obradovich, about 60, Chicago; John E. Stranich, 32, Chicago; Paul D. McKee, 37, Chicago, and Al Heron, Chicago.

2 STILL MISSING

Still missing are Sam Kovarick and David Olson, both of Chicago.

In Johnston Municipal Hospital are Edwin Selvick, 47, of Des Plaines, Ill., whose father was one of the drowned; Capt. Marty Walsh, 64; John O'Connor, 52; Harold Hermansen, 56; Gerald Lesch, 20, Patrick McHale, 55, and Ragnvald Kvaas, 33, all of Chicago.

Released after treatment at County Emergency Hospital were Bernard Selvick, 30, of

The Connell stayed with the scow and later, with the help of the Fucik, secured lines to for the rocks south of the Milwaukee breakwater.

ALL MEN ON DECK

All men aboard the dredge were on the windswept deck of the platform shortly before it capsized since it was impossible to sleep in the rough seas.

In the pitch darkness no one bothered to give the order to abandon ship after the bucket of the big boom swung wildly in the wind.

"There wasn't time," Boehme said.

MATTER OF MINUTES

"The dredge was shipping water faster than we could get rid

DREDGE 906 *headlines from the* MILWAUKEE SENTINEL *on May 24, 1956.*

The tug crew looked behind them and suddenly noticed that the dredge's lights were missing. Staring hard, they saw a flashlight blinking in the water. Their tow cable seemed to be leading down. The tug captain ordered the cable run off the drum and the tugboat turned around and returned to where the dredge had been. The tug's radio did not work, so they could not call for help. The tug captain used his searchlight to locate the cries coming from the water and picked up the crew, one after another.

The tug got its radio working and called a MAYDAY to the Port Washington Coast Guard. Hearing the radio distress call, the nearby 293', 2,447-gross-ton steamer, *Samuel Mitchell,* offered assistance, which was declined for fears of consequences of this larger vessel in the dark waters filled with men in lifejackets. Scattered wreckage, which included hatch covers, chairs, oil drums, and doors, was tossed around by the powerful, 12-foot-high waves.

Unable to locate any more men, and all voices from the water being silenced, the tug requested permission to leave the area and take the survivors to shore for hospitalization and treatment. A Coast Guard boat met the tug returning from the scene. Both vessels proceeded to the Coast Guard base where waiting ambulances took the 13 dredge crew members to a Milwaukee hospital. Three of the 13 were dead on arrival. Later when the sun rose, the Coast Guard recovered four bodies early that morning. Two of the crew were still missing and presumed drowned when the Coast Guard filed the report of its investigation eight days later.

Nine men lost their lives, seven of them definitely by drowning and exposure, and the other two probably from the same causes, although their bodies were never recovered. Captain Walsh survived, as did second-in-command Edwin Selvick, although Selvick's 64-year-old father, one of the crew, did not.

The Coast Guard investigation included remarks that pointed a finger of guilt at Captain Martin Walsh for failing to transfer the 19 men to shore at Oak Creek, and for ordering the dredge to be towed all the way to Milwaukee in the open waters of Lake Michigan during rough weather.

The drowning of the nine men from *Dredge 906* was the second marine tragedy to hit the Milwaukee area within 12 hours. Two fishermen drowned during that storm when their boat capsized inside the breakwater off E. Bennett Ave.

The wreck of *Dredge 906* is one of Milwaukee's most popular scuba dive sites. The dredge rests upside-down on its crane in 55' of water, with the top of the wreck rising to 30'. The silt stirs up easily, so use extreme caution if you are poking around inside; shipwreck penetration diving is still for the specially trained, experienced, and prepared.

ABOVE: DREDGE 906 *is upside-down in 55' of water, so there are opportunities galore to explore underneath a shipwreck.* PHOTO BY JERRY GUYER. BELOW: *Over the years, a clay bank has formed around the outside of the dredge. Two bitts attached to a corner of* DREDGE 906 *hang upside-down just off the lake bottom.* PHOTO BY JON ZEAMAN.

Ellsworth, Colonel

(#6 on the map on p. 269)

VESSEL NAME:	COLONEL ELLSWORTH
RIG:	three-masted schooner
DIMENSIONS:	137' 8" x 26' x 11' 8"
LAUNCHED:	May, 1861; Euclid, Ohio
DATE LOST:	Wednesday, September 2, 1896
CAUSE OF LOSS:	collision with schooner EMILY B. MAXWELL
CARGO:	none
LIVES LOST:	none
GENERAL LOCATION:	18 miles west of Mackinaw City, Michigan
DEPTH:	70' - 85'
ACCESS:	boat
DIVING SKILL LEVEL:	intermediate-advanced
DIVING HAZARDS:	depth, penetration, silting, hypothermia
CO-ORDINATES:	Lat/Lon: 45.48.70 / 85.00.99
	Loran: 31317.4 / 48067.7

Some say that the schooner, *Colonel Ellsworth,* lived a lucky, charmed life, but the bottom line is that she stranded, collided with other ships, and sank when her people didn't want her to strand, collide, or sink!

The *Colonel Ellsworth* was unfortunate and fortunate on a number of occasions: The ship spent the winter of 1867-68 on a cold beach near Alpena, Michigan, on Lake Huron after having stranded there on December 1, 1867. in November, 1868, the schooner ran aground near Lake Huron's Forty Mile Point, but freed herself, suffering minor damage. She was party to a minor collision with another ship outside Green Bay, Wisconsin, in May, 1870. She grounded and sank in Lake Erie near Point Abino on June 8, 1872, but was raised on June 17, 1872, and repaired, and in September, 1875, she stranded along Lake Superior's shores near Calumet, Michigan, but was released with minor damage. In the late fall of 1895, the *Colonel Ellsworth* again stranded on Lake Superior's shores, this time near Whitefish Point, and she spent the winter there before being released in the spring of 1896. She tallied up one expense after another.

Finally, at 4:00 A.M., Wednesday, September 2, 1896, the *Colonel Ellsworth* encountered her final misfortune. While downbound light (carrying no cargo) through the Straits of Mackinac, she collided with the slightly larger 156', Chicago-owned schooner, *Emily B. Maxwell,* loaded with alabaster, and

The three-masted schooner, COLONEL ELLSWORTH *(137' 8" x 26' x 11' 8", 327 gross tons), resembled this ship, the three-masted schooner,* ALICE *(142' x 30' 9' 9", 307 gross tons). The* ALICE, *built at Manitowoc, Wisconsin, in 1881, was abandoned in the Gulf of Mexico in 1930.* AUTHOR'S COLLECTION.

sank, bow first, within 30 minutes in 85' of water. Her crewmembers, escaping in their lifeboat, were picked up by the *Maxwell* and conveyed to shore safely at Mackinaw City. The *Maxwell* was leaking somewhat, but her pumps were keeping her afloat, and she was repaired soon after the collision and returned to service. The *Emily B. Maxwell* ended her career dashed to pieces along Cleveland's breakwall in Lake Erie on August 31, 1909.

The *Colonel Ellsworth's* master, Captain Estell, blamed the "thick weather" for the ships' lookouts not being able to see any lights and for each ship "striking on the bow." At the time of sinking, the *Colonel Ellsworth* was reportedly owned by C.A. Chamberlin of Detroit.

The *Ellsworth's* masts stuck out above the water like telltales marking the wreck site, and hardhat diver John Dodd from Cheboygan, Michigan, salvaged the schooner's anchors, among other items. As was often the custom of government chartmakers early in the 1900's (and a practice worth reviving), this shipwreck was marked by name and type of vessel on the Straits of Mackinac chart.

Launched in May of 1861, right at the beginning of the Civil War, at Euclid, Ohio, the three-masted schooner, *Colonel Ellsworth* (official #4354), was built by William Treat for Charles Hickox of Cleveland. The 327-gross-ton ship measured 137' 8" in length, 26' in beam, and 11' 8" in draft.

The wreck of the schooner, *Colonel Ellsworth,* sits in 85' of water, but rises to about 70' (15' off the bottom), about 18 miles west of Mackinaw City, four miles northeast of the Waugoshance Light, and six miles east of the White Shoals Light.

Located by Chicago shipwreck hunter, Dick Race, in the spring of 1968, the *Colonel Ellsworth* sits upright and intact, with stern damage likely done when the ship hit the hard bottom. The deck in the stern area was pushed up, and the deck housing is missing, likely blown off by the air pressure resulting from the sudden displacement by water when the ship sank. The bow area is also somewhat collapsed.

Items of interest to visiting scuba divers include a windlass at the bow, various deck fittings, and a mast sitting on the lake bottom off the port bow side of the wreck.

Some penetration diving is possible at this site by trained, experienced, and prepared scuba divers, but the silt below deck stirs up all too easily with barely a fin kick. Caution is always advised in shipwreck penetration scuba diving.

Gillen, Edward E.

(#7 on the map on p. 269)

VESSEL NAME:	EDWARD E. GILLEN; ex- ERASTUS C. KNIGHT
RIG:	diesel tugboat
DIMENSIONS:	56' 5" x 15' 3" x 7' 9"
LAUNCHED:	1908; Buffalo, New York
DATE LOST:	Wednesday, June 3, 1981
CAUSE OF LOSS:	capsized
CARGO:	none
LIVES LOST:	none (from 4 on board)
GENERAL LOCATION:	2.5 miles east of Hoan Bridge, Milwaukee
DEPTH:	62' - 74'
ACCESS:	boat
DIVING SKILL LEVEL:	advanced
DIVING HAZARDS:	depth, penetration, silting, hypothermia
CO-ORDINATES:	Lat/Lon: 43.01.50 / 87.49.15
	Loran: 32981.4 / 49283.8

The old, 56', 47-gross-ton tugboat, *Edward E. Gillen,* was helping the 286' U.S. Coast Guard cutter, *Westwind,* in a strain and pull test of the cutter's towing winch just off Milwaukee on Wednesday, June 3, 1981. The wire parted suddenly, and the tug rolled over and sank at 11:47 A.M.

That is the simple story behind the creation of one of Milwaukee's newest dive sites. As usual, there is a lot more than meets the eye and ear.

The *Gillen's* crew of four was plucked from the water immediately by a Coast Guard lifeboat, given first aid in the Coast Guard's sick bay, and then, as an added precaution, transferred to a local hospital for observation. The four had all been wearing lifejackets and suffered only from mild exposure. The wind was calm, but the water was only 48 degrees. The Gillen Company claimed that a replacement tug would cost between $150,000 and $250,000. They had no plans to salvage the old *Gillen.*

The tug sits in 74' of water and is such a small vessel that she can be explored thoroughly on a single tank of air. The pilothouse remains intact, as does the engine room. Be forewarned that only divers trained, experienced, and prepared for penetration diving should enter this little shipwreck.

This steel-hulled steam tug was constructed at Buffalo, New York, in 1908 by Benjamin L. Cowles for Frank P. Coyle of Erie, Pennsylvania. She was launched as *the Erastus C. Knight* (official number 205312), receiving her first inspection on June 29, 1908. Her high pressure, non-condensing engine came from the 1893 steamer, *Mary* (official number 120927).

The *Erastus C. Knight*, owned by the American Sand and Gravel Company of Erie, PA from 1912 until 1918, was renamed *Aubrey* in 1918 when she was sold to the American Construction Company of Cleveland. In the spring of 1928, the *Aubrey's* old steam engine was removed and replaced with a 150 horsepower, six-cylinder Winton-Diesel marine engine, which reduced the tug's fuel costs by two-thirds as she towed a variety of barges around Cleveland.

The 73-year-old tug, EDWARD E. GILLEN, *sank off Milwaukee in 1981 in 74' of water, quickly becoming a very popular scuba dive site.* GREAT LAKES MARINE COLLECTION OF THE MILWAUKEE PUBLIC LIBRARY/WISCONSIN MARINE HISTORICAL SOCIETY.

In 1949, the *Aubrey* was owned by the Merritt-Chapman Scott Corporation. The tug was rebuilt in 1953. In 1958, she was acquired by the Edward E. Gillen Company of Milwaukee, which renamed the little ship the *Edward E. Gillen* in 1964, after their other tug of the same name was decommissioned. The *Gillen* towed construction equipment and barges to a variety of jobs and sites around Milwaukee and other Lake Michigan harbors. The *Gillen* was doing something out of the ordinary when she sank in 1981. In May, 1983, the Edward E. Gillen Company filed a lawsuit against the federal government for $250,000, alleging that negligence on the part of the Coast Guard personnel caused the *Gillen* to sink.

The tug, *Edward E. Gillen,* lies only about a half mile northwest of the wreck of the *Prins Willem V.*

ABOVE: *Below deck on the small tug,* EDWARD E. GILLEN, *trained and experienced scuba divers can explore the galley, complete with a four-burner stove and shelves.* BELOW: *Folding bunkbeds on one side of the tug's pilothouse are a rare sight on a shipwreck, as well as the electric fan on the right side.* PHOTOS BY JON ZEAMAN.

Hackley, Erie L.

(#8 on the map on p. 269)

VESSEL NAME:	ERIE L. HACKLEY
RIG:	wooden steamer
DIMENSIONS:	79' x 17' 4" x 5' 2"
LAUNCHED:	August 11, 1882; Muskegon, Michigan
DATE LOST:	Saturday, October 3, 1903
CAUSE OF LOSS:	foundered in a storm
CARGO:	general merchandise
LIVES LOST:	11 (of 19 on board: 12 passengers, 7 crew)
GENERAL LOCATION:	Green Bay, Wisconsin
DEPTH:	99' - 112'
ACCESS:	boat
DIVING SKILL LEVEL:	advanced
DIVING HAZARDS:	depth, penetration, silting, hypothermia
CO-ORDINATES:	Lat/Lon: 45.03.71 / 87.27.37
	Loran: 32209.5 / 48058.2

Eleven people perished and five of them were not recovered when this small steamer sank in 1903 in Green Bay, Wisconsin, but the physical remains of two of these unfortunate victims were buried on land after considerable controversy 85 years later. Antique kerosene lanterns radiated bright flames from the sides of the turn-of-the-century horsedrawn hearse as the pallbearers, donned in top hats and bow ties, quietly laid these two unidentified victims to their final earthly rest in Bayside Cemetery at Sturgeon Bay, Wisconsin.

Frank Hoffman, who had succeeded in raising the intact schooner, *Alvin Clark*, from 105' of Green Bay water in July, 1969, and who had opened this century-old oddity to the public as a museum (only to have the ship slowly disintegrate by the early 1990's due to insufficient funds for proper conservation), directed salvage to raise the steamer, *Erie L. Hackley*, in 1981. The efforts failed, but two male skeletons were recovered in hopes that surviving relatives would claim the remains. A dilemma arose when no takers appeared.

Legal difficulties prohibited reburying the remains at sea or keeping them in storage at the Door County museum, so Davis Mortuary stored the bones at no charge in the interim. That company donated the wooden coffin and the hearse, the Bayside Cemetery provided the gravesite and its care, and local firms paid for the digging, a burial vault, flowers, and a tombstone.

The 79' ERIE L. HACKLEY *sits in 112' of water.* GREAT LAKES MARINE COLLECTION OF THE MILWAUKEE PUBLIC LIBRARY/WISCONSIN MARINE HISTORICAL SOCIETY.

Built at Musekgon, MI, in 1882, this wooden passenger and freight ship spent her entire career on Lake Michigan. On October 3, 1903, the 79' *Erie L. Hackley* foundered in a squall north of Green Island, Green Bay. The ship (valued at $2,500), her cargo of general merchandise (worth $500), and 11 lives (value: irreplaceable), among them the captain, were all lost while the vessel was enroute from Menominee, MI, to Egg Harbor, WI. The next day, eight survivors were picked up by the passing steamer, *Sheboygan*, after clinging to a deck covering for 14 hours. The ship's cabin washed ashore several days later, with all life belts in place, indicative of the vessel's sudden, unexpected sinking.

Frank Hoffman located the remains of the *Erie L. Hackley* in the summer of 1980 and raised numerous artifacts, such as 36 ink bottles (most of them full), spoons, an iron, and a saw for local museums. But the ship stayed in 110' of water. Today she is an oft-visited site, in part due to her tragic story. The ship's engine, boiler, many artifacts, and a cargo of red bricks are still in place.

When the two skeletons were buried on May 10, 1986, the clergyman who officiated at the graveside ceremony made the occasion a memorial to the victims of the *Hackley* and to the "hundreds of sailors from Door County who perished in Great Lakes shipwrecks."

Frank Hoffman's salvage work ended sadly in dust with the schooner, *Alvin Clark*, but he helped put respectable closure to two human lives in the case of the steamer, *Erie L. Hackley*.

Ironsides

(#9 on the map on p. 269)

VESSEL NAME:	IRONSIDES
RIG:	wooden steamer, twin screw (propeller)
DIMENSIONS:	218' 8" x 31' 7" x 12' 9"
LAUNCHED:	Saturday, July 23, 1864; Cleveland, Ohio
DATE LOST:	Monday, September 15, 1873
CAUSE OF LOSS:	foundered in heavy seas
CARGO:	grain, flour, pork, and sundries
LIVES LOST:	21 (of 50 on board: 18 passengers, 32 crew)
GENERAL LOCATION:	4 miles southeast of Grand Haven, Michigan
DEPTH:	109' - 122'
ACCESS:	boat
DIVING SKILL LEVEL:	advanced
DIVING HAZARDS:	depth, silting, hypothermia
CO-ORDINATES:	Lat/Lon: 43.02.903 / 86.19.138
	Loran: 32525.20 / 49494.50

The 218' 8" *Ironsides*, a misnomer as the vessel was built of wood, slid down the launchramp in Cleveland, Ohio, at 4:00 P.M., Saturday, July 23, 1864, and slide beneath the waves of Lake Michigan four miles off Grand Haven, Michigan, 19 years later just before noon on Monday, September 15, 1873, with the loss of almost half the lives from the 50 that were aboard.

Running from Milwaukee to Grand Haven with a crew of 32, 18 passengers, and half a cargo of freight, much of it in barrels, the *Ironsides* steamed into one of the worst storms of the season. The ship had left Milwaukee at 9:30 P.M. on September 14, 1873, and at 6:00 A.M. the next day, as the vessel approached her destination, Captain Sweetman observed, with increasing stress, the number of schooners and barges, five ships in all, that were stranded ashore on either side of the narrow Grand Haven harbor opening. The *Ironside's* starboard midship gangway had been stove in by waves at 4:00 A.M., and the vessel was taking on water at an alarming rate. The people on board, however, remained eerily calm. The passengers all sat in the main salon, wearing life-jackets in anticipation of the worst. Captain Sweetman decided against attempting to enter the harbor, and turned his ship around into the open lake to ride out the storm. At about 9:30 A.M., the *Ironsides* became unmanageable when rising waters below deck extinguished the fires in the boilers, the vessel ceased her forward motion, and stuck in a trough at the mercy of the wind and the seas.

The wooden steamer, IRONSIDES, *foundered with great loss of life on September 15, 1873, off Grand Haven, Michigan.* GREAT LAKES MARINE COLLECTION OF THE MILWAUKEE PUBLIC LIBRARY/WISCONSIN MARINE HISTORICAL SOCIETY.

Captain Sweetman ordered the American flag run upside-down --- the international distress signal. Hundreds of people had gathered along the shore observing the plight of the various vessels, but were helpless to come to the aid of the stricken *Ironsides*. Sweetman hurried below deck to assess the situation, only to find his crew in waist-deep water pumping futilely to expel the fluid invader. At that point, he knew for sure that his ship would sink. He gave the order to "abandon ship."

It may come as a surprise, this tragedy occurring four decades before the *Titanic* sank with insufficient lifeboats to save everyone, that the *Ironsides* had more than enough lifeboats to accommodate the 50 people on board. Five of the eight boats were launched, but only one reached shore, the others being overturned by the mountainous waves near the shoreline. Some people survived the capsizings; in all, six of the 18 passengers survived, and 23 of the 32 crew. In one heart-wrenching aftermath incident, the body of a five-year-old boy from the *Ironsides* was found half buried in the sand dressed in a little sailor suit. Captain Sweetman, the last to leave the sinking ship, also perished.

The stern of this shipwreck, with its twin propellers and rudder, rests intact in 109' of water, while the broken up bow sits in 122'. The two hogging arches sag towards the center of the hull in midship, and rise above the boilers piping, and engine. The story of the *Ironsides* is one of tragic loss of life, while the shipwreck site today offers incredible views of material history.

Lumberman

(#10 on the map on p. 269)

VESSEL NAME:	LUMBERMAN
RIG:	three-masted schooner
DIMENSIONS:	126' 5" x 23' 5" x 7' 1"
LAUNCHED:	July, 1862; Grand Haven, Michigan
DATE LOST:	Friday, April 7, 1893
CAUSE OF LOSS:	capsized during a squall
CARGO:	none
LIVES LOST:	none (from 5 on board)
GENERAL LOCATION:	off Milwaukee, Wisconsin
DEPTH:	55' - 70'
ACCESS:	boat
DIVING SKILL LEVEL:	advanced
DIVING HAZARDS:	depth, penetration, silting, hypothermia
CO-ORDINATES:	Lat/Lon: 42.52.06 / 87.45.45
	Loran: 33026.4 / 49400.0

This 31-year-old schooner, built at Blendon Landing, part of Grand Haven, Michigan, in 1862, was valued at only $3,000 by 1893. Remarks in the insurance statements indicated that large repairs had been made on this little ship in 1878, 1879, and 1889, and that she was insured only for lumber cargoes, a freight conducive to buoyancy.

On her first trip of the 1893 season, the *Lumberman* left Chicago, where she had wintered, on April 7th, to pick up a load of lumber at Kewaunee. Shortly after the vessel had sailed north past Racine, Wisconsin, the wind picked up. Captain Voss and two sailors were napping below, and the remaining two sailors on deck could not shorten sail fast enough. The light schooner capsized.

Captain Voss and the two sailors below deck, caught quite by surprise, almost went down with the ship, emerging from the cabin just in time before the vessel sank. Voss was also temporarily snagged in the rigging of his sinking ship, faced with the threat of being taken to the bottom with it. The ship sank too fast, carrying the yawl boat down with it. The capsized ship fortunately righted herself during her descent, leaving her telltale masts towering above the water. The five men desperately swam towards these poles and clung to them as their only means of survival.

By luck, they did survive. The steamer, *Menominee*, steamed past the wreck site at about 6:00 P.M. and, noticing the masts, changed direction for a closer look. They found the half-dead, exhausted crew clinging to the cross-trees and conveyed them to Milwaukee. The schooner was considered too old to bother salvaging, although her masts were removed by a tug because they posed a hazard to navigation.

The three-masted schooner, LUMBERMAN, *was apparently camera shy. The vessel above is the schooner,* CARRIER, *similar to the* LUMBERMAN. *The 187-ton* CARRIER *measured 128' 3" x 26' x 8', while the 159-ton* LUMBERMAN *measured 126' 5" x 23' 5" x 7' 1". The* CARRIER, *built in 1865 at Marine City, Michigan, was sold as a houseboat at Chicago in 1914 and disappeared from records.* AUTHOR'S COLLECTION.

The *Lumberman* was located on July 16, 1983, by Dan Johnson, president of a salvage firm in Rockford, IL, who went to court for ownership of all artifacts from the vessel and sought financial backing to raise the ship (the *Alvin Clark* had not yet fallen apart to teach us what happens when we raise shipwrecks from Great Lakes waters.)

Today, the wreck of the schooner, *Lumberman,* is still a dive site. She sits upright and intact in 70' of water, with her decks rising to about 55'. Her deck is relatively intact, with a capstan in place. Penetration of this ship's hull through her cargo holds from bow to stern is relatively easy for divers with good shipwreck penetration training and skills.

This is a classic beauty of a shipwreck in a comfortable depth.

Maitland

(#11 on the map on p. 269)

VESSEL NAME:	MAITLAND
RIG:	three-masted bark (barque)
DIMENSIONS:	133' 7" x 25' 9" x 11' 6"
LAUNCHED:	1861; Goderich, Ontario
DATE LOST:	Sunday, June 11, 1871
CAUSE OF LOSS:	bizarre collisions with the schooners, GOLDEN HARVEST and MEARS
CARGO:	corn
LIVES LOST:	none
GENERAL LOCATION:	7.1 miles west of Old Mackinac Point, MI
DEPTH:	70' - 85'
ACCESS:	boat
DIVING SKILL LEVEL:	advanced
DIVING HAZARDS:	depth, penetration, silting, hypothermia
CO-ORDINATES:	Lat/Lon: 45.48.29 / 84.52.39
	Loran: 31273.1 / 48092.7

Built at Goderich, Canada West (now Ontario), on the eastern shores of Lake Huron, by Henry Marlton in 1861, the three-masted bark, *Maitland,* plied Great Lakes waters for only ten years before sinking in an unusual set of collisions in the Straits of Mackinac on Sunday night, June 11, 1871.

The *Maitland* cleared Chicago on Friday, June 9, 1871, with 18,000 bushels of corn bound for Buffalo. By Sunday night, June 11, 1871, she was approaching the Straits of Mackinac for the transition from Lake Michigan to Lake Huron. She never made that crossing.

A *Maitland* lookout sighted the lights of a schooner approaching them directly on a collision course at about 10:00 P.M. on a clear, fog-free, slight-breeze night. Captain Brown ordered the *Maitland* steered hard to port (left) in an attempt to avoid a collision. The move came somewhat too late. The *Maitland* and the approaching schooner, which turned out to be the *Golden Harvest,* glanced off each other starboard to starboard, but not without snagging rigging. The *Maitland's* bowsprit and starboard anchor caught the *Golden Harvest's* rigging and sailed away with it so forcefully that both of the *Golden Harvest's* masts crashed down, fatally injuring the second mate who suffered a skull fracture. Another man on the *Harvest* broke a leg, while the wheelsman broke several ribs. The *Maitland's* bowsprit broke off during the encounter.

That damage to both vessels was bad enough, but not enough to sink a ship. Unfortunately, the *Maitland* had not seen the OTHER schooner that was running behind and a bit off the starboard side of the *Golden Harvest*. This was the vessel, *Mears,* which sliced neatly and directly into the *Maitland's* wooden hull on the starboard bow, her vulnerable side while she continued her hard-to-port turn after her brush with the *Golden Harvest*.

The *Mears* split her bow stem and lost some headsail equipment, but the *Maitland* sank within five minutes from the fatal impalement. The *Maitland's* crew hastily took to their yawl boat and rowed towards the lights of nearby Mackinac City, where they arrived safely. The *Mears* was towed to Chicago by the tug, *Magnet,* and repaired. The 421-gross-ton, 172' schooner, *Mears,* built in 1869, ended her career when she stranded and broke up north of Au Sable, Michigan, on Lake Huron, on November 27, 1889, with the loss of one life. The 255-gross-ton *Golden Harvest* received a tow to Racine, Wisconsin, by the wrecking tug, *Leviathan,* and was also repaired at a cost of $9,800. She had been built at Buffalo in 1856 and was reportedly still in commission over 40 years later. Around that time, the aging *Golden Harvest* was likely quietly abandoned in some Great Lakes backwater.

The 252-gross-ton *Maitland* measured 133' 7" in length, 25' 9" in beam, and 11' 6" in draft at the time of loss. She had passed to U.S. ownership on October 19, 1866. Canadian measurements had the ship listed as 137' 10" in length simply because of different reference points from which to measure being used between Canada and the U.S. In May of 1868, the *Maitland* was seized at Detroit by a tug commandeered by a revenue agent who accused the ship of sailing under the U.S. flag while being a British (Canadian) vessel. It took a day to clear up this misunderstanding.

Features at this shipwreck site include the stub of the bowsprit (which had broken off when it snagged in the *Golden Harvest's* rigging), along with a bilge pump, samson posts, and a windlass. The collision gash created by the *Mears'* bow is immediately to the starboard side of the foremast hole, which still sports a portion of railing around where the mast stood. The expensive masts and rigging were salvaged by the famous Great Lakes wrecker, Captain Peter Falcon, two weeks after the *Maitland* sank.

The *Maitland* sits in 85' of water, with the starboard gunwale rising to a depth of 70', while the port gunwale is situated at 76'. In the middle of the ship is the centerboard winch, while the stern displays the cabin outline, the rudder post, and the rudder itself turned hard to port, frozen forever in its final defensive posture trying to avoid what its crew thought was a single collision.

Below deck, the silt is light but very deep. Although it is possible to swim most of the length of the *Maitland* below deck, the probability of stirring up the silt to the point where visibility is zero is quite good. Remember that penetration shipwreck diving takes special training, experience, and preparation.

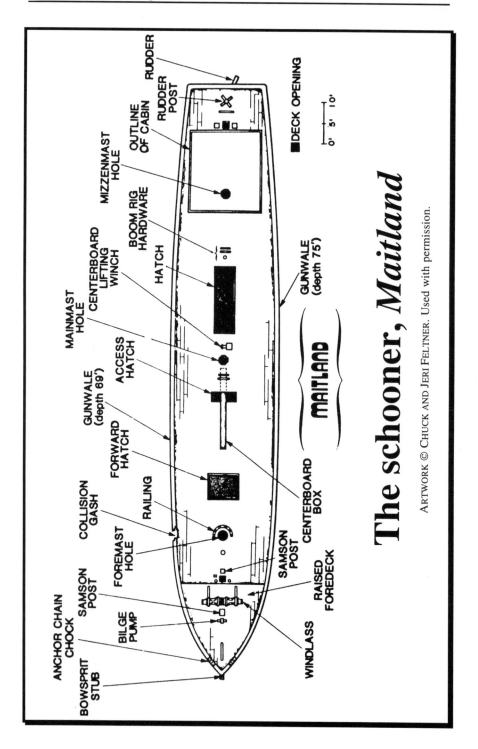

The schooner, *Maitland*

ARTWORK © CHUCK AND JERI FELTNER. Used with permission.

Material Service

(#12 on the map on p. 269)

VESSEL NAME:	MATERIAL SERVICE
RIG:	barge
DIMENSIONS:	239' 7" x 40' 1" x 13' 9"
LAUNCHED:	1929; Sturgeon Bay, Wisconsin
DATE LOST:	Wednesday, July 29, 1936
CAUSE OF LOSS:	foundered
CARGO:	sand and gravel
LIVES LOST:	15 (from total of 22 on board)
GENERAL LOCATION:	2000' NE of Calumet Harbor Light, Illinois
DEPTH:	22' - 38'
ACCESS:	boat
DIVING SKILL LEVEL:	novice-intermediate
DIVING HAZARDS:	penetration, silting, fishing lines, boat traffic
CO-ORDINATES:	Lat/Lon: 41.44.50 / 87.30.50
	Loran: 33426.3 / 50201.4

Before the pre-dawn glow of a glorious midsummer day, the sand and gravel barge, *Material Service*, weighed down by 2,000 tons of crushed stone it was transporting from the Chicago River south to the Calumet River, lurched sharply to port, as if hitting something, and sank so suddenly that there was no time to give the alarm. Fifteen men, including the captain and the chief engineer, from the 22 crew on board lost their lives because they were trapped in their berths below deck.

The specially-designed, canal-sized motorship, *Material Service*, was equipped with twin, six cylinder diesel engines, twin screws, and self-loading and unloading machinery. Her twin engines were served by twin rudders. Her low superstructure permitted her to pass under the low clearance roadway bridges which span the Chicago River. Built of steel in 1929 at Sturgeon Bay, Wisconsin, for Chicago's Material Service Corporation (founded in 1919 to supply sand and gravel to the Chicago area), any bridge superstructure was virtually non-existent, consisting only of a basic, shallow pilothouse at the stern. This area included the crew's accommodations.

The ship's short history was not without alarming incident. Allegedly, jealous business rivals of the Material Service Corporation planted the nitroglycerin or dynamite which rocked the ship on November 30, 1930, killing one man and injuring several others. No conclusion was ever reached.

The uniquely designed barge, MATERIAL SERVICE, *operated for seven years with ease in passing under low bridges in Chicago. Sadly, when she sank, her low pilothouse became an inescapable coffin for several men.* GREAT LAKES MARINE COLLECTION OF THE MILWAUKEE PUBLIC LIBRARY/WISCONSIN MARINE HISTORICAL SOCIETY.

The *Material Service* provided several years of excellent service to her owners. Then came the early morning of July 29, 1936, the last day in the ship's and several sailors' lives. At 1:00 A.M. on this conventional run to the Calumet River, the ship's second engineer noticed two feet of water, increasing rapidly, in the engine room's bilge. He started first one, then a second, bilge pump. At that point, the ship lurched suddenly to port and was quickly swamped by the heavy seas. Powerful torrents of water gushed into the hatchways, preventing any human movement against them in the crew's frantic efforts to escape this steel coffin. Eleven of the 22 on board actually freed themselves from the hull, but four of these were yanked under by the powerful suction of the sinking ship, which went down within one minute in almost 40' of water.

Only the removable A-frame of the self-unloader and the bow light staff protruded from the water. The Coast Guard at the Calumet station rescued four of the men, the tug, *New Jersey*, picked up two more, and a seventh man swam to the Calumet lighthouse and was pulled to safety. However, 15 of their fellow crewmembers were dead, launching an immediate investigation into the sinking.

The controversy over the cause of the sinking raged on long after the bodies were recovered from the wreck. One theory, supported by the ship's owners, was that the *Material Service* was caught in a trough between two waves, slammed her hull onto Calumet Shoal, ruptured her hull plates, flooded and sank. But the officially supported theory was that the ship's captain, Charles D. Brown, in spite of 37 years of sailing experience, was negligent in failing to order tarpaulin covers fastened over the hatch covers. This allowed water to saturate the cargo and make the load too unwieldy and heavy, leading to the sinking. This theory found the most support from among the shipwreck survivors, so the lake tragedy was blamed upon the late captain.

Three days after the sinking, hardhat divers recovered nine of the 15 bodies, including Captain Brown's. Six corpses had been in the wreck, while three were a short distance off. A total of 13 of the 15 bodies were eventually recovered. The A-frame and light staff were removed and replaced by a temporary buoy marking the shipwreck site.

Attempted salvage of the ship over the next ten years failed. A Canadian company tried for two years in the early 1940's to raise the vessel, without success. In 1944, a Detroit man purchased the *Material Service* hulk for $3,250 in hopes of raising the ship or salvaging the engines; his efforts also failed.

Scuba divers have explored this shipwreck for years. One newspaper article from July, 1961, stated that "Although the 240-foot vessel has been below the surface for nearly 25 years, [the divers] are still finding equipment intact." The news item went on to list the things which were found and removed from the wreck: two large wrenches, a porthole cover, cups and saucers, the ship's telegraph, a bottle of hair oil, and several electric fans. It is not known where these artifacts are today, what condition they are in, or how many of them have been trashed because they could not be properly conserved. One can also be curious about the gold watch which was reportedly found in the springs of what had once been a bed on the *Material Service.*

In the late 1970's, some Chicago area scuba divers, viewing the stern's below-deck access as a strong candidate for a scuba fatality, dynamited that part of the shipwreck to make penetration impossible. Many divers and charter boat operators condemned this as needless destruction.

The wreck lies in Indiana waters and is marked by buoy "WR10." It is illegal to tie a boat to a government buoy, so anchor next to the wreck. The average visibility is low --- 7 feet. The ship's huge holds are wide open, with gravel cargo, but there is enough room to explore below deck for the trained and prepared. The damaged stern reveals exposed pipes, buckled plates, fragmented metal, and the aft deck and crew's quarters scattered. The propellers are still in place, although half buried in the lake bottom.

One closing fact: Four of the 15 drowned men were from Sturgeon Bay, WI, where the ship was built in 1929. The buoy placed on the *Material Service* in August, 1936, broke free and was found almost a year later, 250 miles away, at Sturgeon Bay, WI. To get into the bay, the buoy had to enter the narrow mouth of the Sturgeon Bay ship canal. Such is the spectral strength of kinship.

Milwaukee (#13 on the map on p. 269)

VESSEL NAME:	MILWAUKEE; launched as MANISTIQUE, MARQUETTE & NORTHERN NO. 1
RIG:	steel railroad ferry steamer
DIMENSIONS:	338' x 56' x 19' 5"
LAUNCHED:	December 6, 1902; Cleveland, Ohio
DATE LOST:	Tuesday, October 22, 1929
CAUSE OF LOSS:	foundered
CARGO:	railroad cars
LIVES LOST:	all hands (52)
GENERAL LOCATION:	7 miles NE of Milwaukee, 3 miles offshore
DEPTH:	90' - 125'
ACCESS:	boat
DIVING SKILL LEVEL:	advanced
DIVING HAZARDS:	depth, penetration, silting, entanglement
CO-ORDINATES:	Lat/Lon: 43.01.69 / 87.40.44
	Loran: 32943.4 / 49208.8

The autumn of the year 1929 is best remembered in general history as the time of the Stock Market Crash in late October which dramatically began the ten-year-long, worldwide Great Depression of the 1930's. While the year 1929 has become a symbol of financial disaster, that year is recalled by Great Lakes veterans for its marine tragedies on Lake Michigan.

Almost 100 people lost their lives in the sinking of four ships on Lake Michigan late in 1929. The 267' steel steamer, *Andaste*, disappeared with the loss of 25 lives on September 9, 1929 (see page 471). The steamer, *Wisconsin*, went down with the loss of nine live and 59 people saved off Kenosha, Wisconsin, on October 29, 1929 (see pages 347-350). On October 31, 1929, the automobile freighter, *Senator*, sank in a collision about 20 miles off Port Washington, Wisconsin, with the loss of seven lives (see p. 472).

The worst of the four disasters occurred on October 22, 1929, when the Grand Trunk car ferry, *Milwaukee*, sank somewhere off Milwaukee with all hands, a total of 52 lives.

The 338', steel *Milwaukee* departed from its namesake city at about 12:30 P.M. bound for Muskegon, Michigan, with a cargo of 27 loaded freight railroad cars. A gale was raging out of the northeast when the ship cleared the breakwater, but her captain, nicknamed Robert "Heavy Weather" McKay for his tendency to sail in any weather in order to keep to his schedule, was determined to reach his destination. No one ever saw the ship afloat again, nor any of the 52 people on board alive again. It was later learned that the ship had foundered some time not long after 6:30 P.M. on the day she left Milwaukee.

This archival view of the steel car ferry, MILWAUKEE, *seen here leaving Grand Haven, Michigan, for Milwaukee, Wisconsin, in 1910, 19 years before she sank with the loss of 52 lives, shows two railroad boxcars and the stern area which was damaged during the furious Lake Michigan storm on October 22, 1929.* AUTHOR'S COLLECTION.

Several days later, the freighter, *Colonel*, brought wreckage floating in the lake likely from the *Milwaukee* into port, ending hopes that the vessel had survived the storm. A floating pilothouse with the name, *Milwaukee*, clearly on it was seen by another ship. Two bodies wearing *Milwaukee* lifejackets were brought in to harbor; one carried a watch which had stopped at 9:35. Members of the South Haven (Michigan) Coast Guard located a battered tin can floating near the beach. It contained a water-soaked, barely legible note, written in pencil, signed by A. R. Sadon, the ill-fated *Milwaukee's* purser. It read, "S.S. Milwaukee, Oct. 22 --- '29 6:30 P.M. Ship is taking water fast. We have turned and headed for Milwaukee. Pumps are all working, but sea-gate is bent and won't keep water out. Flickers *[nickname for the crew's quarters]* are flooded. Seas are tremendous. Things look bad. Crew roll about same as last pay day."

That message, short yet descriptive, was all that anyone heard from the *Milwaukee*. Although the year was 1929, the ship carried no wireless (radio) equipment on board, and so was unable to transmit an S.O.S. signal. Sailors along Milwaukee's waterfront were betting that the railroad cars had shifted in the swelling seas, popping out of their on-board, iron railroad tracks and being thrown towards one side of the ship, causing the vessel to capsize and sink.

Three crewmembers were lucky. They felt so positive that the inclement weather would keep the *Milwaukee* from sailing that day that they lounged around the headquarters of the seamen's union for most of the afternoon. After all, gale warnings had been posted since 8:30 that morning, and none of the other railroad car ferries put out of Milwaukee that day. When the sailors finally returned to their ship, they discovered that the vessel had sailed. Their initial embarrassment and frustration turned into overjoyed relief at being alive when they later learned that their ship was lost with all hands.

The *Milwaukee*, built at Cleveland, Ohio, and launched in late 1902, sported not one, but two, triple expansion steam engines, and a total of six boilers. In the fall of 1908, the ship was sold to the Grand Trunk, Milwaukee Car Ferry Line, and on December 1, 1908, her original, unwieldy name, *Manistique, Marquette & Northern I*, was changed simply to *Milwaukee*.

One boxcar on the MILWAUKEE *contains a cargo of bathtubs .* PHOTO BY JON ZEAMAN.

The remains of the car ferry, *Milwaukee*, located in April, 1972, by well-known shipwreck hunters John Steele and Kent Bellrichard on a commercial fishermen's tip, lie upright in 125' of water, sitting in sand and mud, and rising to about 90' off the bottom due to the ship's height, about seven miles northeast of Milwaukee and three miles off shore. The engine controls were found in the

"Stop" position, indicative of an action which would allow the crew to launch the lifeboats. The ship, however, apparently sank so fast that only one lifeboat was released from its davits. Divers found that the railroad boxcars had, indeed, left their tracks, shifted to one side of the ship, and damaged the sea gate. This allowed water to quickly seep into the vessel.

The low visibility, usually 15' or less, and the maze of tangled wires and twisted cables make this a potentially dangerous dive. Divers can explore the broken superstructure of this shipwreck, and see many of the railroad cars, since this area is open. A couple of the railroad cars can be explored: one contains a cargo of old bathtubs and toilet seats, while another holds three automobiles. Disorientation is very possible at this site, since the ship is split in places, with gaps and tangled wreckage between main hull portions. In some areas, the silt is three feet deep and stirs up easily, causing no-visibility situations. A hole cut into the engine room by an early salvor allows a view of one of the twin engines, with a variety of tools scattered about. The stern gate, with its storm damage which caused the ship to sink, is quite evident. The twin propellers are also still visible in place. Beware of darkness (take a light), silt-out conditions, entanglement possibilities, and occasionally strong currents. Very experienced divers with proper training, conditions, and equipment, can enter the shipwreck.

The name above this shipboard doorway reveals its identity. PHOTO BY JON ZEAMAN.

Morazan, Francisco

(#14 on the map on p. 269)

VESSEL NAME:	FRANCISCO MORAZAN; launched as ARCADIA
RIG:	ocean-going, steel freighter
DIMENSIONS:	246' 9" x 36' 10" x 16' 8"
LAUNCHED:	1922; Hamburg, Germany
DATE LOST:	November 29, 1960
CAUSE OF LOSS:	stranded
CARGO:	lard, hides
LIVES LOST:	none (from 16 on board)
GENERAL LOCATION:	off SW corner of South Manitou Island, MI
DEPTH:	0' - 20'
ACCESS:	boat
DIVING SKILL LEVEL:	novice
DIVING HAZARDS:	silting
CO-ORDINATES:	Lat/Lon: 44.59.07 / 86.08.09
	Loran: 31858.5 / 48339.3

Business concerns in the Great Lakes have dreamed, since at least the 1850's, of becoming actively involved in the international trade of the world, sending ships overseas with North American cargoes, while welcoming saltwater ships with foreign products. Quite a few vessels with low draft could pass through the Welland Canal and interconnecting locks in the St. Lawrence River since the mid-1800's, but the ships and cargoes were usually too small to make this a profitable, full-time route. It was not until the completion in 1959 of the much-debated and long-constructed St. Lawrence Seaway that Great Lakes ports became part of the sailing schedules of many larger ships which usually sailed only the oceans of the world. Some of these vessels unfortunately became permanent Great Lakes features. The German ship, *Nordmeer* (see *The 100 Best Great Lakes Shipwrecks, Volume I*, pp. 187-189), stranded on Lake Huron rocks in 1966 and remains there to this day. The same happened to the Liberian freighter, *Francisco Morazan*, on Lake Michigan shoals in 1960.

Built at Hamburg, Germany, in 1922 by Deutsche Werft A.G., this 1,412-ton steel ship was launched as the *Arcadia*, renamed the *Elbing* in 1934, renamed the *Empire Congress* in 1945, renamed the *Brunes* in 1946, renamed the *Skuld* in 1947, renamed the *Ringas* under Norwegian registry in 1948, renamed the *Los Mayas* in 1958, and finally renamed the *Francisco Morazan* in 1959.

The ocean-going steamer, Francisco Morazan, *was named the* Ringas *when the ship first visited the Great Lakes in the early 1950's.* Great Lakes Marine Collection of the Milwaukee Public Library/Wisconsin Marine Historical Society.

This 247' ship first visited the Great Lakes in 1953 as the *Ringas*, prior to the opening of the St. Lawrence Seaway, and she entered the inland seas again in each of the shipping seasons of 1958, 1959, and finally, 1960.

After loading a cargo of hides, canned chicken, shampoo, and other products at Chicago, the *Francisco Morazan* attempted to leave the Great Lakes before the close of the St. Lawrence Seaway in late November, 1960. Captained as his first command by a young (26-year-old) Greek captain named Eduardo Trizizas, who originally thought that he had a week before the Seaway closing date, but then found out he had only three days, he poured on the power in his haste to reach the open ocean towards his goal, Rotterdam, Holland. Captain Trizizas, trying to sail as direct a line as possible from Chicago to the Straits of Mackinac, overlooked the obstacles called islands, and the *Francisco Morazan* ran aground on rocks just southwest of South Manitou Island, several miles off Michigan's mainland shoreline on November 29, 1960.

The *Morazan* was hopelessly grounded in about 15' of water, and had unintentionally crushed the 1903 wreck of the wooden steamer, *Walter L. Frost*, the remains of which lie a few hundred feet south of the *Morazan*. The Coast Guard removed the crew two days later before worse weather set in, and the vessel was turned over to Roen Salvage Company of Sturgeon Bay, Wisconsin, which could not free the steel ship before her hull cracked and she became unsalvageable. Most of the cargo, however, was removed.

The U.S. Coast Guard removed the crew of the MORAZAN *in early December, 1960, when approaching storms posed a safety threat.* GREAT LAKES MARINE COLLECTION OF THE MILWAUKEE PUBLIC LIBRARY/WISCONSIN MARINE HISTORICAL SOCIETY.

The crew of this Liberian-registered ship included the captain's pregnant, 29-year-old wife and 14 Cuban, Spanish, and Greek sailors, six of whom immediately encountered problems with U.S. immigration officers because they were subject to deportation as "undesirable" aliens due to criminal records, health problems, or previous records of jumping ship. They were escorted to New York City to make certain they left the country. The others were taken to New York by bus so they could return to their respective homes.

The *Francisco Morazan* is the most visited shipwreck in Michigan's Manitou Underwater Preserve because a dramatic, conspicuous profile of the rusting ship still towers high above the shallow water, making it a target for curious boaters as well as scuba divers. About 800' off the island, the wreck requires a boat for a visit, and boaters usually tie off to the shipwreck or anchor just off the hull. The above-water superstructure, rusting out and slippery with seagull guano from birds who have made it a nesting ground, is dangerous to explore. Below water, the hull is broken and sand-filled, but the considerable stern machinery makes this a rewarding dive. Jagged steel edges and occasional oil leaks can make this site damaging to scuba equipment, so use caution here.

When you view these corroding shipwreck remains of the ocean-going *Francisco Morazan*, remember that the Great Lakes' involvement in world trade came fraught with danger as well as profit.

Niagara

(#15 on the map on p. 269)

VESSEL NAME:	NIAGARA
RIG:	sidewheel steamer
DIMENSIONS:	245' x 33' 6"
LAUNCHED:	1845; Buffalo, New York
DATE LOST:	Wednesday, September 24, 1856
CAUSE OF LOSS:	burned
CARGO:	personal items of passengers
LIVES LOST:	at least 60 (from about 300 on board)
GENERAL LOCATION:	7 miles NE of Port Washington, Wisconsin
DEPTH:	42' - 57'
ACCESS:	boat
DIVING SKILL LEVEL:	intermediate
DIVING HAZARDS:	silting, disorientation, boiler penetration
CO-ORDINATES:	Lat/Lon: 43.29.19 / 87.46.55
	Loran: 32800.2 / 48988.5

The loss of the steamer, *Niagara*, is considered the seventh worst disaster on Lake Michigan in terms of loss of life. At least 60 people (some reports give the number as being over 100!) perished when this wooden vessel burned and sank in what was perhaps a case of arson.

This nine-year-old steamship, one of the many vessels busy transporting new pioneer families to the western frontier away from the corruption inherent in the big cities on the East Coast at that time, had departed Collingwood, Ontario (then called Canada West), under fair conditions at 9:00 P.M., September 22, 1856. Captain Frederick Miller, besides being in charge of his ship and crew, was responsible for the 300 passengers, 21 horses, and 105 tons and several wagons of freight and baggage on board. The passengers, many representing entire families, carried everything they owned in the world with them. Gold was the only currency trusted by common folk at that time, so several people carried their wealth around their waists in money belts.

Enroute, the ship made stops at Mackinac, Two Rivers, Manitowoc, and Sheboygan, unloading cargo and disembarking passengers at each stop, as well as taking on new freight and people. The *Niagara* was steaming south towards Port Washington, Wisconsin, at 4:00 P.M. on September 24, 1856, when flames and smoke suddenly emanated from above an aft stovepipe. Captain Miller, upon seeing the smoke, immediately ran to the pilot house and ordered the ship headed towards shore. Unfortunately, the engine expired, and the vessel drifted helplessly miles off shore. At that point, crew members were busy performing a variety of emergency tasks. Some manned the pumps in an effort to extinguish the flames. Others with axes hacked doors and deck planks, and threw these items overboard for later use as floats by people in the cold water when the ship finally disappeared beneath the waves.

The terror-stricken passengers panicked. The thick smoke, the frantically working crew, and the screams emanating from some of the passengers drove the rest of them into a state of frenzy. Some immediately plunged into the lake, drowning within minutes. Many who remained on board burned to death, while some lost consciousness from smoke inhalation and suffocated. Only one lifeboat was launched from the stern, with several children being added to the already fully loaded boat with 22 people in it. Once it was launched, more desperate passengers tried to jump into it from the blazing ship, only to capsize the lifeboat and drown everyone except the very few who ended up clinging to the bottom of the boat. Those passengers who climbed into the ship's rigging perished when smoke inhalation weakened them and knocked them down, or burned to death when they fell into the flames, or drowned when the masts finally burned through and collapsed into the lake. Many people in the water clung in thick clusters to ropes trailing from the doomed ship. One line, with five women despairingly clinging to it, burned through at the ship's railing. All five drowned. Ropes were attached to the guard rails at the stern and let down, and a large number of people, mostly women and children, slide down those ropes and hung there in clusters, clinging to each other, until the ropes were burned off. Some tried to cling to a spar in the water, but most were drowned. Despite assistance from five nearby ships which raced to the scene of the black plume of smoke, over 60 people from the *Niagara* died that day.

The cause of the fire was never definitely ascertained, but it could have originated from an overheated funnel casing. A more ominous story was told by Captain Miller (who had done much to soothe the panic and save lives, and who had been the last to leave the burning *Niagara)* in a letter he wrote and sent to the CHICAGO TRIBUNE. Apparently there had been frequent dissatisfaction on the part of some emigrants bound to Green Bay, who found themselves unable to reach that place by direct route, and were either left at Mackinac or brought up the lake. Miller wrote:

"...on leaving Collingwood, we had quite a number of those disaffected ones, and while lying at the dock, the steward, Mr. Clark, found in his room, on his desk, the following letter, and handed it to me:

"'LOOK OUT! ---Save yourself, the boat will be burned tonight; everything is in readiness, we have made ample preparations to take care of ourselves. (Signed) A PASSENGER.'

"I immediately called the engineer, Mr. Leonard, into my room, showed him the letter, and also Captain Dick, of the lower lake steamer *Peerless;* when after a consultation, we concluded to set a strict watch, but yet without showing any signs of alarm. My wheelsmen were constantly traveling around the boat, but saw nothing that would lead them to suspect any person. Every fear, therefore, died away, and we thought nothing more of the matter.

"Now, I am confident that the boat did not take fire from the machinery, nor from the boilers, as every portion of her fire-hold was fire proof. My opinion is, that the fire was caused by some combustible material stowed under the shafts, but the nature of which we were unable to tell, as packages frequently come so disguised that we cannot tell what they are; but it must have been something of that kind from the fact that it enveloped the boat in flames almost instantly; and when first discovered, it was impossible to subdue it.

"I cannot, at present, write more, as I am now on the eve of leaving the city to return to the wreck, nor do I think more is necessary.

Fred. Miller, Late Master Steamer *Niagara"*

The 1,100-ton, 245', wooden paddlewheel steamer, *Niagara*, was built at Buffalo, New York, in 1845, making her the earliest constructed vessel in the "100 Best Shipwrecks" list. She missed being the earliest sinking by four days: the brig, *Sandusky* (see pp. 326-331), sank in a storm at Mackinac on Sept. 20, 1856, while the *Niagara* burned on September 24, 1856. The *Niagara* carried paddlewheels which were 30' in diameter and which powered her vertical beam engine with the aid of two 65-inch cylinders, a ten-foot stroke, and three boilers.

The *Niagara* experienced two close calls in her career before her final demise. On September 3, 1847, lost in a fog while approaching the Straits of Mackinac from the east, the ship ran aground off Bois Blanc Island. A passing steamer paused to pull her off, with only slight damage to the stranded vessel. Later, in November, 1851, the *Niagara* collided with the 258-ton brig, *Lucy A. Blossom*, in the Detroit River, with the sailing ship, valued at $10,000, quickly sinking, her crew rescued by the steamer.

The historic *Niagara* lies in 57' of water about two miles off Harrington Beach in the town of Belgium, Wisconsin, seven miles northeast of Port Washington, Wisconsin. This tragic sinking has been described as the eleventh worst Great Lakes shipping disaster in terms of loss of life.

The wreck and her cargo lie broken up and scattered, with the bow facing towards shore. Much of the keel, ribs, and machinery remain, with the hull broken into two large pieces and its sides fallen outward. The diamond-shaped walking beam and engine rise 15' off the bottom. One paddlewheel is intact, with the other one quite damaged. The massive boilers, another impressive wreck sight, lie north off the wreck, often with a line leading divers to them from the main wreckage. A visit to this site will not disappoint divers!

Norlond

(#16 on the map on p. 269)

VESSEL NAME:	NORLOND; launched as EUGENE C. HART
RIG:	wooden, propeller-driven freighter
DIMENSIONS:	152' 5" x 25' x 9' 4"
LAUNCHED:	Friday, June 27, 1890; Manitowoc, WI
DATE LOST:	Monday, November 13, 1922
CAUSE OF LOSS:	foundered in heavy seas
CARGO:	general merchandise: toys, pharmaceuticals
LIVES LOST:	none (from 20 on board)
GENERAL LOCATION:	3 miles southeast of St. Francis, Wisconsin
DEPTH:	48' - 58'
ACCESS:	boat
DIVING SKILL LEVEL:	intermediate
DIVING HAZARDS:	depth, visibility, darkness, silting
CO-ORDINATES:	Lat/Lon: 42.58.35 / 87.48.69
	Loran: 32999.8 / 49320.5

The 522-ton, 153', wooden freight and passenger steamer, *Norlond* (often incorrectly called the *Norland* in modern, as well as contemporary, accounts), slid down Manitowoc's launch ramp in the early summer of 1890, christened the *Eugene C. Hart*, and worked on the Great Lakes and the East Coast for over 32 years. Official number 136131, this vessel was initially used for service between Green Bay and Mackinac Island, and later between St. Joseph, Michigan, and Chicago.

On October 26, 1917, the *Eugene C. Hart* was sold to a company in Hartford, Connecticut, on the East Coast, for use there during World War I. The ship was renamed the *Norlond* in 1919 and stayed in service, enrolled in New York, NY, on the Atlantic Coast until returning to the Great Lakes in the spring of 1922, purchased by the Chicago and Milwaukee Steamship Company. That year was destined to be the vessel's final year of service, and it seemed as though she was returning to her region of birth to meet her death.

On Saturday, November 11, 1922, the *Norlond* left Chicago at 11:00 P.M. with a huge cargo of toys, plumbing supplies, and pharmaceutical items, valued at an overwhelming half a million dollars at that time. The wind and waves were picking up, so the ship put in at Racine, Wisconsin, early on Sunday, November 12th for shelter. There the crew found several leaks which had sprung during the pounding on the lake. They quickly patched up these leaks as best as possible in order to get them to Milwaukee, their cargo's destination, another 25 miles north. The storm had subsided enough by Monday morning, November 13th, that the *Norlond* departed Racine 11:40 A.M.

This early photograph depicts the wooden steamer, EUGENE C. HART, *later renamed the* NORLOND, *departing Green Bay. The* NORLOND *sank in 58' of water on November 13, 1922, with no loss of life.* GREAT LAKES MARINE COLLECTION OF THE MILWAUKEE PUBLIC LIBRARY/WISCONSIN MARINE HISTORICAL SOCIETY.

The temporary leak repairs, however, failed to hold, and the crew pumped water furiously out of the holds. Before long, the *Norlond* listed heavily in this losing battle, and the captain ordered the two lifeboats lowered, with ten crew filling each boat. Less than half a minute after the second lifeboat was launched, the *Norlond* disappeared to the lake bottom. The high winds and rolling waves had again increased in speed and size, but the men rowed for their lives until the two lifeboats safely reached the shore. The *Norlond,* however, lay in 58' of water eight miles shy of her destination.

During the summer months of 1923, the small wrecking steamer, the *Jane,* salvaged most of the cargo of merchandise, as well as the ship's engine. After that, the *Norlond* lay forgotten for many years.

Jump 37 years into the future from the time of the *Norlond's* sinking. In 1922, commercial radio was just in its early stage, black-and-white silent films were the norm in movie theaters, while hardhat diving was still a very traditional occupation on the Great Lakes. By 1959, most homes in the United States had a television set, color films with quality sound were standard productions in Hollywood, and there were, by far, more scuba divers doing explorations of the inland seas than hardhat divers, who represented an activity, if not a breed of human, that seemed to be rapidly dying out.

Modern wreck hunter John Steele, just beginning his four-decade-long string of Great Lakes shipwreck discoveries, located the remains of the steamer, *Norlond,* in 1959, 37 years after the ship sank, in 58' of water three miles southeast of the town of St. Francis, Wisconsin.

In such relatively shallow water, the upper portion of the ship's hull had completely fallen apart, leaving the keel, boiler, gear box, prop shaft, and propeller in open view. The boiler, the highest profile point of this basically two-dimensional shipwreck, rises about 10' off the sand and mud bottom of the lake. Many interesting smaller items can be found and viewed at this popular shipwreck site.

OLD SHIP SINKS IN ANGRY LAKE

Crew Escapes as Waves Send $500,000 Cargo to Bottom.

Milwaukee, Nov. 14—After being buffeted by a heavy storm for two hours and springing four large leaks

The headlines and lead for the loss of the NORLOND, TOLEDO BLADE, *Nov. 14, 1922.*

O'Connor, Frank

(#17 on the map on p. 269)

VESSEL NAME:	FRANK O'CONNOR; ex-CITY OF NAPLES
RIG:	wooden steamer
DIMENSIONS:	301' x 42' 5" x 22' 8"
LAUNCHED:	Sat., Sept. 17, 1892; West Bay City, MI
DATE LOST:	Thursday, October 2, 1919
CAUSE OF LOSS:	burned
CARGO:	coal
LIVES LOST:	none (21 on board)
GENERAL LOCATION:	off Cana Island, Wisconsin
DEPTH:	50' - 67'
ACCESS:	boat
DIVING SKILL LEVEL:	intermediate
DIVING HAZARDS:	variable visibility, slight current
CO-ORDINATES:	Lat/Lon: 45.06.80 / 87.00.77
	Loran: 32078.8 / 48115.8

A red glow dominated the evening sky over Lake Michigan along Door County's eastern shoreline on October 2, 1919. The wooden steamer, *Frank O'Connor*, was ablaze.

The *Frank O'Connor* was launched as the *City of Naples* at West Bay City, Michigan, in 1892, and at 301' in length, was one of the largest freighters on the Great Lakes at the time. She was rebuilt in 1904 and renamed in 1916.

The *O'Connor* loaded 3,000 tons of coal at Buffalo, New York, on September 29, 1919, and headed for Milwaukee, Wisconsin, almost 1,000 water miles away. Four days later, the steamer was abeam of Cana Island, Wisconsin, when the dreaded cry of "FIRE!", accompanied by the sudden, frightful, non-stop sound of bells, startled everyone on board into action. The watchman had discovered smoke streaming from one of the aft hatches.

Hatch covers were removed in an attempt to locate the source of the fire, but thick, billowing smoke drove back the men on deck. Air currents wafted into the open hatchways, and soon, soaring flames replaced the smoke. The water hoses seemed like Davids battling Goliaths.

Captain William J. Hayes soon realized that his ship would burn to the waterline, so he ordered the sea cocks opened to hasten the *O'Connor's* sinking.

Then all hands were ordered to abandon ship. They quickly rowed towards nearby Cana Island Lighthouse, and before they reached their destination, they paused to watch and hear the illuminating fire from their ship hiss in extinguishing anguish while the steamer plunged to the dark, cold bottom of the lake. The Bailey's Harbor Coast Guard Station crew safely removed the 21 tired and shaken crew members. The press reported that the ship went down in 17 fathoms (102').

The steamer, FRANK O'CONNOR, *burned in 1919.* GREAT LAKES MARINE COLLECTION OF THE MILWAUKEE PUBLIC LIBRARY/WISCONSIN MARINE HISTORICAL SOCIETY.

The wreck of the *Frank O'Connor* was located in 67' of water in late 1990 by Sam Mareci and Tom Beaudwin. Within a year, Chicago scuba divers had illegally removed one of the ship's anchors. Several outraged Wisconsin divers, recognizing the anchor's historical and recreational value, reported the offenders to police, and, after charges were laid, an out-of-court settlement drafted by the Door County District Attorney was accepted. The defendant had to surrender the anchor, which he had placed as ornamentation at his cottage, and move it to the Cana Island Lighthouse, where it remains on display overlooking the site where its ship met its end.

The *Frank O'Connor* sits upright with most of her artifacts and much machinery, including the 20' 1,100 horsepower triple expansion steam engine and two 13' boilers, still in place. There are also a steam windlass, a capstan, and a 12' propeller. The shipwreck is in incredible condition, considering that she burned (the early scuttling undoubtedly did much to maintain the good condition of the wreck), and the site has been described as "a mini-museum of nautical engineering."

ABOVE: *The mechanical components, such as engine controls, of the steamer,* FRANK O'CONNOR *can still be appreciated by visiting divers.* BELOW: *The 12', four-bladed propeller is one of the highlights of a visit to this site.*   PHOTOS BY JON ZEAMAN.

Sandusky

(#18 on the map on p. 269)

VESSEL NAME:	SANDUSKY
RIG:	brig
DIMENSIONS:	110' x 25' 1"
LAUNCHED:	1848; Sandusky, Ohio
DATE LOST:	Saturday, September 20, 1856
CAUSE OF LOSS:	foundered
CARGO:	grain
LIVES LOST:	all hands (7)
GENERAL LOCATION:	5.1 miles west of Old Mackinac Point, MI
DEPTH:	70' - 84'
ACCESS:	boat
DIVING SKILL LEVEL:	advanced
DIVING HAZARDS:	depth, penetration, silting
CO-ORDINATES:	Lat/Lon: 45.48.09 / 84.50.08
	Loran: 31262.0 / 48100.9

On September 23, 1856, a Milwaukee newspaper announced: "There is a report that a brig has foundered in the Straits [of Mackinac] with all hands lost." The report was correct, the vessel was the *Sandusky*, and all seven men on board died in the sinking.

The Straits of Mackinac, also called the crossroads of the Great Lakes because that is the point where Lakes Huron and Michigan meet (with Lake Superior not very far away), form a relatively narrow channel through which sailed or steamed all of the ships that provided the swelling masses of immigrants and pioneers for Chicago, Milwaukee, and the far Midwest, and most of their supplies. In view of the intense and dense marine traffic through the Straits since the mid-1800's, it comes as no surprise that dozens of shipwrecks dot the bottom profile.

The brig, *Sandusky,* represents the earliest sinking on the Great Lakes in this listing of "The 100 Best Great Lakes Shipwrecks," narrowly (by four days) beating out the second earliest, namely another Lake Michigan wreck, the steamer, *Niagara* (see pp. 260??-262??), which sank on September 24, 1856 (although the *Niagara* is the oldest, built in 1845). The *Sandusky,* built at Sandusky, Ohio, in 1848, was not issued an official number because that system of registering ships did not come into use until after the Civil War. The 225-gross-ton (old measure) *Sandusky* was 110' long and 25' 1" wide.

The brig, SANDUSKY, *was probably never photographed, considering her early lifespan (1848-1856), but she undoubtedly would have resembled this unidentified, old, foreign visitor to the Great Lakes, photographed in about 1900, flying the flag of Puerto Rico. The last U.S. brig to sail the inland seas was supposedly the* ROBERT BURNS, *which sank in the Mackinac area on Nov. 17, 1869.* AUTHOR'S COLLECTION.

The *Sandusky* was used early in her career as a grain carrier running between Buffalo and Chicago, a distance she could cover in seven days, which was faster than the average sailing ship at that time. The *Sandusky,* however, was accident-prone. In October of 1848, her first year afloat, she stranded on Lake Erie's notorious Long Point, but was pulled off. She sprang a serious leak on June 16, 1851, and had to retreat to Buffalo. On September 3, 1851, she stranded on a Lake Erie reef, and only the jettisoning of some of her cargo released her. In June, 1855, she stranded on Lake Michigan's Beaver Island, again having to jettison her cargo to free herself.

New owners acquired the *Sandusky* in September, 1856, much to the chagrin of two of her crew, Irishmen Samuel McQue and Charles O'Shea, who secretly left the vessel in a desertion attempt at Chicago. They must have been under contract as indentured servants, because they were arrested by the police and released to the custody of the *Sandusky's* captain, who ordered them back aboard. Ironically, when the *Sandusky* sailed on her final voyage, she carried these two very unwilling sailors who had been legally shanghai-ed on this trip into eternity.

The *Sandusky* departed Chicago on September 16, 1856, reaching the northern end of Lake Michigan two days later, simultaneously with a violent gale. The *Sandusky* never arrived at Buffalo, and no survivor ever staggered ashore to tell the tragic tale of the ship's loss, so precisely what happened to her is vague and speculative. One ship reported seeing a vessel believed to be the *Sandusky* sink, with her crew clinging desperately to the masts, but was incapable of reaching them. The sidewheel steamer, *City Queen,* reported trying unsuccessfully to rescue three sailors clinging to a spar in the Straits.

With the loss of seven lives, the *Sandusky* ranks as one of the worst disasters in the Straits of Mackinac. Only the *Cedarville*, which sank in 1965 with the loss of ten lives (see *The 100 Best Great Lakes Shipwrecks, Volume I,* pp. 145-148), and the as-yet-unlocated brig, *Robert Burns,* which foundered in 40' of water three miles east of Bois Blanc Island in Lake Huron on November 17, 1869, also with ten lives lost, rank worse.

Located by Chuck and Jeri Feltner and their team of scuba divers on May 2, 1981, the *Sandusky* sits upright and mostly intact in 84' of water a little over five miles west of Old Mackinac Point. This shipwreck was totally intact when scuba divers, the first people to see this ship in 125 years, first explored her. Unfortunately, since her location became public knowledge and many divers converged on this site, numerous deadeyes and belaying pins have gone missing, the ship's wheel has been broken, and the unique and ornate scroll figurehead was so damaged in a theft attempt in July, 1988, that it was removed to the Michigan Maritime Museum in South Haven for safekeeping, conservation, and display. Since the summer of 1989, a replica figurehead, commissioned and placed by Detroit area divers, adorns the bow of the *Sandusky.*

Diver Sharon Troxell examines the original scrolled "ramshead" figurehead on the wreck of the brig, SANDUSKY, *on July 3, 1988. Some time during the next four days, unknown divers attempting to steal this figurehead damaged it to the point that it was later removed for protection and conservation. In 1989, a replica figurehead replaced the original. This may be the last photograph taken of the original, undamaged,* SANDUSKY *figurehead.* PHOTO BY CRIS KOHL.

The upright hull, which lists slightly to port, is intact, showing no signs of fire, collision, or ice damage. The single-level deck on this ship shows signs of severe erosion, indicative of having been submerged longer than most known shipwrecks. The silt below deck, measured at over four feet deep, also indicates long submergence. No evident of cargo was located; the *Sandusky* carried perishable grain. Commercial fishing nets from more modern times are snagged on the stern quarters.

The *Sandusky's* bow is the highlight of any underwater exploration of this shipwreck. The scroll figurehead, with some resemblance to a ram's head, is rare, only about a dozen known Great Lakes shipwrecks having carried a figurehead. The cutwater bow, the hinged 21-foot-long bowsprit, and the extensive (42' in total length) jib-boom are still upright and in place. With this headgear arrangement, the *Sandusky* was over 150' long! The bowsprit was hinged to allow vessel passage through Welland Canal locks (which, in the mid-1800's, could accommodate ships no longer than 142' in length).

Also near the bow are the ship's two wooden-stock anchors, anchor chain, a windlass with older-style ratchet pawls, a toppled mast, and a wooden head grating which served a necessary purpose on older ships. In those early days of shipping, it was common practice to have a head grating mounted between the headrails, which were located between the catheads and the figurehead, as a platform upon which sailors could stand and relieve themselves. Since the head grating was located at the head, or front, of the vessel, the term "head" came into common usage referring to the toilet facility on a boat.

Deadeyes, some with rope remnants still in the "eyes" (the use of rope rather than wire being indicative of an older style ship) and wooden belaying pins (rather than hollow iron ones, which were the norm after about 1860) were found in large quantities on the deck of the *Sandusky* initially, but are far fewer in numbers today. At the stern, the highlights are the remains of the ship's wheel, with its rope barrel (a pre-1850 design), and the tiller on the rudder post. A capstan with half a dozen pigeonholes sits on deck near the middle of the wreck, with a centerboard winch nearby. The ship's compass was found in the cabin opening.

Dive on the *Sandusky* and you will explore one of the oldest and best-preserved shipwrecks in the entire Great Lakes, in spite of the site degradation caused by time, extensive visitation, and outright theft.

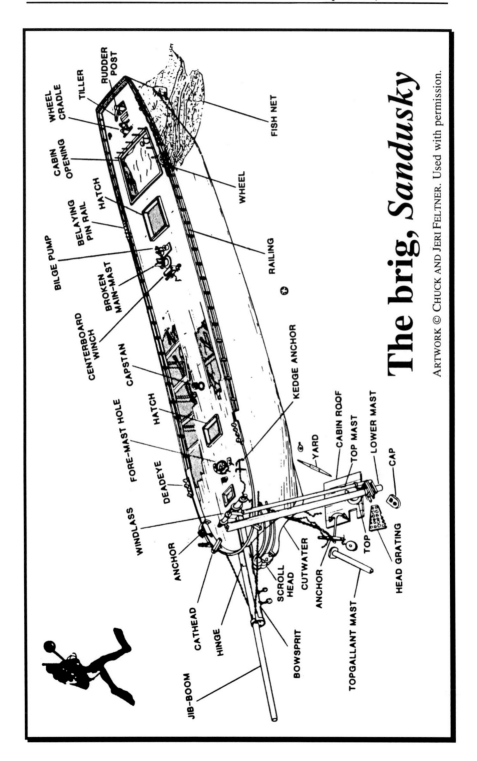

The brig, *Sandusky*

ARTWORK © CHUCK AND JERI FELTNER. Used with permission.

Tacoma

(#19 on the map on p. 269)

VESSEL NAME:	TACOMA
RIG:	wooden, steam-powered tug
DIMENSIONS:	73' 4" x 18' x 9'
LAUNCHED:	1894, Benton Harbor, Michigan
DATE LOST:	Monday, November 4, 1929
CAUSE OF LOSS:	foundered
CARGO:	none
LIVES LOST:	none (from 6 on board)
GENERAL LOCATION:	Chicago's Clark Point Shoal
DEPTH:	27' - 35'
ACCESS:	boat
DIVING SKILL LEVEL:	novice-intermediate
DIVING HAZARDS:	
CO-ORDINATES:	Lat/Lon: 41.46.22 / 87.31.37
	Loran: 33417.7 / 50178.9

The *Tacoma* was a wooden tugboat built in 1894 at Benton Harbor, Michigan, by E. W. Heath for Fitzsimons & Connell Dredge & Dock Company of Chicago.

Measuring 73' 4" in length, precisely 18' in beam, and 9' in draft, this vessel of 76 gross tons (39 net tons) was assigned official number 145673 and received her first inspection on July 3, 1894.

The *Tacoma's* fore and aft compound engine, built by the Montague Iron Works of Montague, Michigan, was capable of producing 450 horsepower, while the ship's single fire box type boiler measured 7.5' deep by 16' long.

The *Tacoma* worked all her life on the waters of Lake Michigan, toiling mostly as a dredge tug.

On Monday, November 4, 1929, the tug, *Tacoma,* at the advanced age of 35 years (old for a wooden vessel on the Great Lakes), foundered in 35' of water near the 68th Street crib in Chicago, about half a mile north-northwest from Clarke's Point Shoal Buoy, and about 2.5 miles 342 degrees from Calumet Harbor Light.

The crew of six saved themselves by jumping aboard a passing scow.

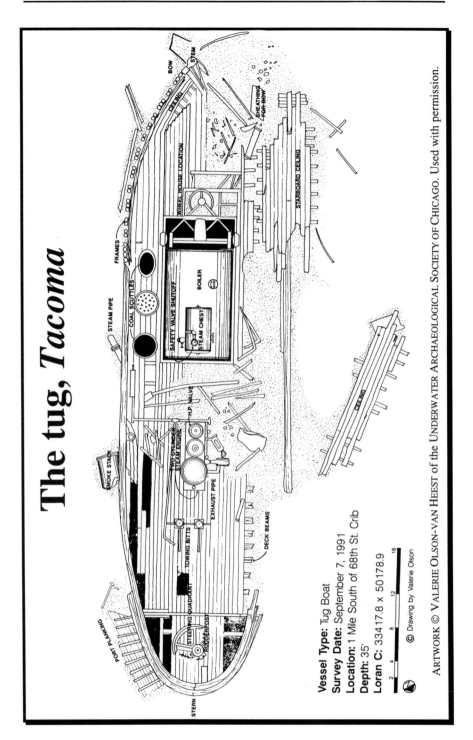

The tug, *Tacoma*

Vessel Type: Tug Boat
Survey Date: September 7, 1991
Location: 1 Mile South of 68th St. Crib
Depth: 35'
Loran C: 33417.8 x 50178.9

© Drawing by Valerie Olson

ARTWORK © VALERIE OLSON-VAN HEEST of the UNDERWATER ARCHAEOLOGICAL SOCIETY OF CHICAGO. Used with permission.

The tug, TACOMA, *spent all of her 35 years plying Lake Michigan waters before foundering in 35' of water on November 4, 1929.* GREAT LAKES MARINE COLLECTION OF THE MILWAUKEE PUBLIC LIBRARY/WISCONSIN MARINE HISTORICAL SOCIETY.

This 1929 shipwreck did not receive much newspaper coverage because a) there was no loss of life in this sinking, b) the vessel was a tugboat rather than a larger commercial ship, c) the vessel was old and virtually worthless, and d) the newspapers were filled with as much information as they could possibly find about the loss of the steamer, *Wisconsin* (see pp. 347-350), on October 29, 1929, with nine lives lost, and the loss of the automobile freighter, *Senator* (see p. 472), with the loss of seven lives on October 31, 1929. These major Lake Michigan shipping losses relegated the story of the *Tacoma* to one or two lines on obscure newspaper pages.

Today, the *Tacoma* sits upright on a sand bottom. When she sank, her pilot house was still attached and had about 20' of water over it, but natural ravages, such as wind, waves, and ice, have destroyed this portion of the shipwreck. Most of the tug, however, remains, with the steam engine accessible due to the absence of decking above the engine compartment.

Another highlight of the *Tacoma* site is the large and very photogenic propeller.

Taylor, Hetty (#20 on the map on p. 269)

VESSEL NAME:	HETTY TAYLOR
RIG:	two-masted schooner
DIMENSIONS:	110' long
LAUNCHED:	
DATE LOST:	Thursday, August 26, 1880
CAUSE OF LOSS:	foundered
CARGO:	none
LIVES LOST:	none
GENERAL LOCATION:	off Sheboygan, Wisconsin
DEPTH:	97' - 107'
ACCESS:	boat
DIVING SKILL LEVEL:	advanced
DIVING HAZARDS:	depth, silting, disorientation, hypothermia
CO-ORDINATES:	Lat/Lon: 43.40.86 / 87.39.31
	Loran: 32700.9 / 48885.5

This newspaper account of the *Hetty Taylor's* sinking, short and to-the-point, appeared in the CHICAGO INTER OCEAN on August 28, 1880:

"Sheboygan, Wis, Aug. 27.---The schooner *Hetty Taylor*, of Milwaukee, from that port, light, bound for Escanaba, was struck by a heavy squall when about five miles off this port, at 11 o'clock last night, and capsized. All hands were saved. The crew came here for assistance, but went back with the tug *Messenger* in search, and found the schooner sunk in fourteen fathoms, and the maintopmast about eight feet out of water."

This account is likely not quite accurate. The 110', twin-masted schooner, *Hetty Taylor*, apparently heading up the Wisconsin coast towards Escanaba, Michigan, to pick up a load of lumber, encountered a severe gale that capsized the ship. The crew abandoned ship in a lifeboat and headed for nearby Sheboygan, Wisconsin. Meanwhile, the *Hetty Taylor* settled with her bow hitting the lake bottom and her stern out of the water. The newspaper account mentioned that the vessel had gone down in 14 fathoms, which is only 84'. Today's underwater explorers will find the *Taylor* in 107' of water.

Five salvage attempts, including one by famed Great Lakes wrecker, Captain Peter Falcon of Chicago, all failed to return the schooner, *Hetty Taylor*.

In the process of attempted recovery, the vessel had her masts snapped off and her stern damaged.

The remains of the *Hetty Taylor* sit upright on a sand bottom, with bowsprit and bow chains in place, but with considerable damage to one side of the hull and the stern. The deck is still in place, for the most part, but disappears into the sand on the damaged side of the hull, where divers can find the intact compass house. The damaged stern still has its rudder in place, buried in the sand. The open cargo holds are of interest, and the undamaged side of the hull has fish painted on the board where the ship's name plate was once attached. One mast lies about 50' off the starboard beam, while numerous deadeyes and other artifacts can be seen at this site.

Although little is known about the history of this particular Great Lakes vessel, much can be seen and appreciated by exploring the schooner, *Hetty Taylor's*, remains.

The schooner, JOSEPH DUVALL, *pictured above, closely resembled the apparently unphotographed schooner,* HETTY TAYLOR. *Both vessels carried two masts, and the* HETTY TAYLOR *was 110' in length, while the* JOSEPH DUVALL *measured 106' 9". The* DUVALL *sank in a collision on the St. Clair River in 1905.*   AUTHOR'S COLLECTION.

Three Brothers (#21 on the map on p. 269)

VESSEL NAME:	THREE BROTHERS; launched as MAY DURR
RIG:	wooden steambarge
DIMENSIONS:	162' x 31' 4" x 11' 8"
LAUNCHED:	1888; Milwaukee, Wisconsin
DATE LOST:	Wednesday, September 27, 1911
CAUSE OF LOSS:	stranded
CARGO:	lumber
LIVES LOST:	none
GENERAL LOCATION:	South Manitou Island, Michigan
DEPTH:	5' - 45'
ACCESS:	shore from the island
DIVING SKILL LEVEL:	novice
DIVING HAZARDS:	silting, disorientation, shifting sands
CO-ORDINATES:	Lat/Lon: 45.00.557 / 86.05.592
	Loran: 31839.28 / 48339.32

The story of the wooden steamer, *Three Brothers*, is unique in that this shipwreck would not have been discovered without the help of Mother Nature, the force which destroyed this ship in the first place.

Built as the steamer, *May Durr*, for the lumber trade in 1888 at Milwaukee, official number 91998, this 162' ship plied the waters for only four years under that name. In 1892, the vessel was renamed the *John Spry*, a designation which lasted for a decade until *Three Brothers* became the ship's new tag.

The three brothers after whom this ship was renamed were all involved in the lumber trade. Born at Owen Sound, Ontario (Canada West) between 1859 and 1863, William, James, and Thomas White established their own lumber company in Michigan in the 1880's. They ran uniquely successful operations at Boyne City, Michigan, and Tonawanda, New York, under the name of William H. White & Company lumber dealership. This steamer, the *Three Brothers*, generally ran between Boyne City and Tonawanda.

On September 27, 1911, however, the *Three Brothers* was bound from Boyne City to Chicago with $4,200 worth of hardwood lumber on her deck. Shortly after departure, the 23-year-old steamer's seams opened and the ship took on water, several feet of it in her holds by the time they passed the lightship at North Manitou Island. At that point, when it became obvious that the pumps could no longer keep the ship afloat, Captain Sam Christopher decided to run his ship ashore at South Manitou Island. With the engine still laboring at full steam, the *Three Brothers* plowed into the sandy shoreline about 600' east of the Lifesaving Station. The pilot house at the bow and the complete deckload of lumber were dislodged by the force of the impact, and the thick stem post split in two. The entire crew was rescued by the men of the Lifesaving Station, minus their personal effects, while the ship sank, bow in 16' of water and the stern settling into 45'. Some basic salvage of anchors and bow capstan took place, but the *Three Brothers* itself was a total loss.

The shipwreck disappeared into the restless sands of Sandy Point Beach on South Manitou Island, and stayed hidden for many years. Scuba divers in quest of this shipwreck in the 1970's and 1980's were stymied at finding only a few planks which they presumed were all that was left of the steamer that had apparently been pounded to pieces.

Years later, on April 30, 1996, employees of Sleeping Bear Dunes National Seashore took a boat to South Manitou Island and began preparations for another season of spring and summer visitors to the popular island. These workers were the first ones to notice that Sandy Point had unexpectedly and totally disappeared over the course of the winter storms, and that a well-preserved shipwreck, clearly visible from above water, had been uncovered in its place.

The *Three Brothers* had come back from the dead after 85 years.

Word of this unique shipwreck discovery spread quickly among the excited Great Lakes scuba diving community. More than 1,000 divers visited the site in 1996, making it the most visited shipwreck in Michigan.

Visitors to this site, which is accessible from the shore once divers reach the island, were not disappointed. The pilot house, upper cabins, and forward half of the decking are missing, a situation to be expected considering the shallow depth of the wreck and the harshness of northern winters, and deck beams near the hatches are fractured, weakening the hull integrity. The stern, however, in the deep end, is amazingly well-preserved. The words, "Three Brothers of Buffalo," are easily readable on the richly-textured wooden transom, while fire hoses snake over the railing and the top (the cylinder head) of the engine is visible above the remaining sand.

The existing sand inside the ship's hull has been allowed to stay put, acting both as a possible resistance to ice and wave damage to the hull, as well as a barrier to artifacts which dishonest divers might be tempted to remove from the site as "tokens of accomplishment" of their visits.

Unfortunately, a very small minority of unscrupulous divers may have betrayed a trust by giving in to these temptations. Brass fire hose nozzles, carved wooden pillars from the ship's stern, brass fittings from the steam engine, and some personal items from the ship's crew were all either stolen by divers or reburied in the sands in 1996. This led to conflict and flailing accusations between marine archaeologists (self-proclaimed and otherwise) and state officials on the one hand, and the scuba diving community on the other, reportedly with threats of shipwreck access limits hurled once more against sport divers.

Three Brothers, Boyne City, Mich.

The steamer, THREE BROTHERS, *worked in the lumber trade until stranding at South Manitou Island with no loss of life on September 27, 1911. This picture appeared on an early 1900's postcard.* GREAT LAKES MARINE COLLECTION OF THE MILWAUKEE PUBLIC LIBRARY/WISCONSIN MARINE HISTORICAL SOCIETY.

There is another problem in the conservation of shipwrecks. Compared to the wanton vandalism of artifact removal or the threat of declaring a shipwreck off-limits to sport divers, the accidental damage done to the shipwreck by modern anchors snagged into it from visiting pleasure craft indeed seems minimal. But it is clear that education of divers and boaters is necessity for shipwreck and artifact survival. As MICHIGAN HISTORY MAGAZINE succinctly put it in 1996, "Artifacts left in place on shipwrecks will draw divers (and their dollars!) for years. Artifacts removed and sold out of state or left to molder in garages benefit few."

The *Three Brothers* sank and disappeared into the sands of Lake Michigan in 1911. The real-life three brothers, William, James, and Thomas White, went bankrupt in 1913 and, dispersing to the sands of the western United States, disappeared into the landscape of history.

The significant physical remains and contents of the steamer, *Three Brothers*, must not disappear, neither to the landscape of nature nor to the whims of man. They are too important for us to lose again.

Verano

(#22 on the map on p. 269)

VESSEL NAME:	VERANO
RIG:	pleasure yacht
DIMENSIONS:	88' 3" x 16' x 8"
LAUNCHED:	1925; Morris Heights, New York
DATE LOST:	Wednesday, August 28, 1946
CAUSE OF LOSS:	foundered
CARGO:	none
LIVES LOST:	all hands (3)
GENERAL LOCATION:	7 miles north of South Haven, Michigan
DEPTH:	50' - 55'
ACCESS:	boat
DIVING SKILL LEVEL:	intermediate
DIVING HAZARDS:	silting, disorientation
CO-ORDINATES:	Lat/Lon: 42.3021. / 86.15. 96
	Loran: 32707.72 / 49843.95

The newspaper headlines screamed about the mysterious sinking of one of the Great Lakes' largest luxury yachts with the loss of all three lives that were on board on August 28, 1946, seven miles north of South Haven, Michigan.

The Coast Guard had approached the apparently abandoned ship found awash off Michigan's shoreline in hopes of attaching a line to the vessel and towing it in to port, but when they were within ten feet of the *Verano*, she sank stern first in about 60' of water. There had been no signs of life on board, and the lifeboat was missing, so it was assumed that the crew had abandoned ship.

J.R. Baumgartner of the Hotel Astor in Milwaukee had sold the *Verano* only two weeks earlier to Maynard Dowell of Park Ridge, Illinois, a Chicago suburb. Baumgartner, president of the Reliable Tool & Machine Company, had owned the ship for several years. Dowell, president of Aero Dusters Inc., an aerial crop-dusting company, had paid $75,000 for the *Verano*, which was on its way to Holland, Michigan, for refitting and repainting at the time of loss.

Dowell, however, was not on board. A Chicago business associate of his, Chester Granath, 43, undertook the delivery job to Holland. With him were a Detroit engineer named Fred Stenning, 37, and a Japanese-American named Ben Murakoshi, 60, the yacht's cook. Granath's wife had waved good-bye to them as the yacht departed Chicago.

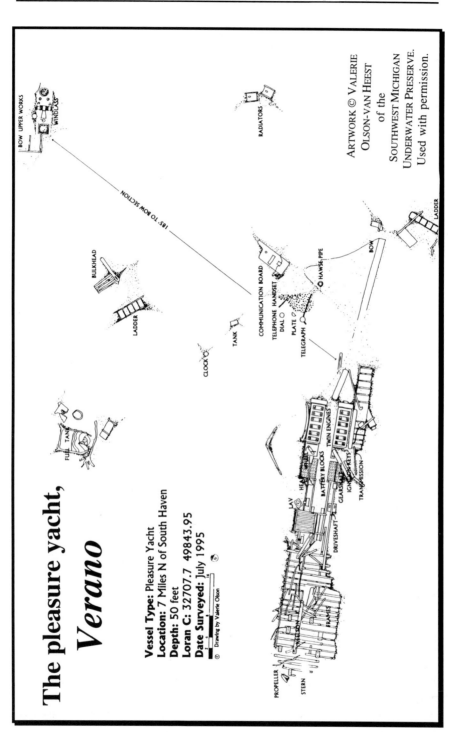

The pleasure yacht, *Verano*

Vessel Type: Pleasure Yacht
Location: 7 Miles N of South Haven
Depth: 50 feet
Loran C: 32707.7 49843.95
Date Surveyed: July 1995

© Drawing by Valerie Olson

ARTWORK © VALERIE
OLSON-VAN HEEST
of the
SOUTHWEST MICHIGAN
UNDERWATER PRESERVE.
Used with permission.

The twin-engined pleasure yacht, VERANO, *was built at the height of the roaring 1920's in New York state, during the same year that the most famous Jazz Age novel,* THE GREAT GATSBY, *was published: 1925.* GREAT LAKES MARINE COLLECTION OF THE MILWAUKEE PUBLIC LIBRARY/WISCONSIN MARINE HISTORICAL SOCIETY.

"I was going to go along," Mrs. Granath reportedly said, "but for some reason, I don't know why, I didn't."

The Coast Guard continued their search on the water, along the shoreline, and from the air. They soon located the *Verano's* floating, overturned lifeboat, with no sign of life, five miles southwest of where the ship sank. The next day, Granath and Stenning were found dead on the shore near the spot where the *Verano* sank. The cook's body was not located until the next year.

The wooden *Verano*, built as the *Idler* in 1925, the height of the roaring Jazz Age, at Morris Heights, New York, by Consolidated Ship Building Corp., measured 92' overall. The ship was renamed the *Paul Reese II* on June 1, 1933, when it changed owners, and was renamed *Verano* on June 17, 1935. Her twin gas engines (4 cycle, 6 cylinder) could produce 600 horsepower.

Two weeks after the sinking, Jack Lyons, of Whitehall, Michigan, bought the rights to the *Verano* and, during a salvage attempt, the ship broke to pieces. These pieces were found by scuba divers Tom Tanczos and Robert Trowbridge in September, 1994, within the boundaries of the proposed Southwest Michigan Underwater Preserve, in 55' of water. The bow and stern sections are 185' apart, but some of the interesting sights include the ship's wheel, windlass, compass, pottery, twin engines, propeller, and the ignition key still in place.

Willem V, Prins

(#23 on the map on p. 269)

VESSEL NAME:	PRINS WILLEM V
RIG:	steel freighter
DIMENSIONS:	250' 5" x 42' 1" x 14' 7"
LAUNCHED:	1940/1948; Hardinxveld, Netherlands
DATE LOST:	Thursday, October 14, 1954
CAUSE OF LOSS:	collision with the tug, SINCLAIR'S, tow
CARGO:	automotive parts, animal hides, jukeboxes...
LIVES LOST:	none (from 30 on board)
GENERAL LOCATION:	3 miles east of Milwaukee, Wisconsin
DEPTH:	48' - 90'
ACCESS:	boat
DIVING SKILL LEVEL:	advanced
DIVING HAZARDS:	depth, penetration, silting, strong currents
CO-ORDINATES:	Lat/Lon: 43.01.36 / 87.48.47
	Loran: 32979.7 / 49286.9

The steel steamer, *Prins Willem V*, is the Milwaukee area's most popular scuba dive attraction. The complete tale of the *Willie*, as this ship is affectionately known to those who explore her often, would encompass an entire book on its own. Here, in a nutshell, is this shipwreck's story.

The keel of this steel ship was laid in 1939 at Hardinxveld, Netherlands (Holland), and she was more than half completed when World War II started. What was built of this ship was scuttled on May 10, 1940, in the new waterway river at Rotterdam to block that waterway's use by the invading German army. In 1945, after the war, the ship was raised, cleaned, and finished, finally going into service in January, 1949, for the Dutch-owned Oranje Line.

The *Prins Willem V* carried cargoes mostly between northern European ports and the Great Lakes, she being just the right dimensions to utilize the old canal system on the St. Lawrence River in these pre-St. Lawrence Seaway days.

On October 14, 1954, the *Prins Willem V,* loaded with a wide variety of cargo which included hides, outboard motors, slabs of pork fat, automotive parts, 10 Wurlitzer jukeboxes, movie projectors, a printing press, twine, musical instruments, lawn mowers, and 230 television tubes, departed Milwaukee at suppertime. Less than a mile outside the harbor, the freighter's captain saw the tug, *Sinclair,* and made a slight course change to avoid the vessel, but failed to see that the *Sinclair* was towing an oil barge at the end of an 800' cable. The *Prins Willem V* cruised headlong into the cable, eventually colliding twice with the towbarge at 7:16 P.M. After the accident, the 1,567-gross-ton *Prins Willem V* limped eastward for another two miles and an hour before the 20' gash in her starboard midship and the hole in her starboard bow proved fatal on this, her 25th voyage to the Great Lakes. The Coast Guard cutter, *Hollyhock*, picked up the 30 crew from their lifeboats. The *Sinclair* and her tow reached port safely. A subsequent board of inquiry ruled both captains to blame for the accident.

The PRINS WILLEM V *was a frequent visitor to the Great Lakes in the years just before the construction of the St. Lawrence Seaway.* GREAT LAKES MARINE COLLECTION OF THE MILWAUKEE PUBLIC LIBRARY/WISCONSIN MARINE HISTORICAL SOCIETY.

The wreck of the *Prins Willem V* sits on a heavy port list in 90' of water, sinking a bit deeper into the sand and clay each year, three miles east of Milwaukee harbor. The wreck rises about 40' off the lake bottom, and anywhere on this enormous site is a good place to begin explorations. The ship's name and home port appear in white letters on the stern. The superstructure, with its intact pilot house, doors and portholes, sits in midship. The bow offers machinery and other interesting items. Divers can also see a huge tank used in a salvage attempt years ago along one side. Enormous cargo hatches are open on deck, revealing some of the cargo still inside. Penetrate this wreck only if properly trained in, and prepared for, such diving. Ironically, no lives were lost when the ship sank in 1954, but several scuba divers have died while penetrating this huge shipwreck. Beware of occasional strong currents and entanglements.

A scuba diver ascends one of the angled masts of the freighter, PRINS WILLEM V, *lying on its port side in about 90' of water off Milwaukee.* PHOTO BY JON ZEAMAN.

ABOVE: *The pilot house of the* PRINS WILLEM V, *although on a port angle with the rest of the shipwreck, is interestingly intact with its doorways and ports.* BELOW: *Inside the engine room, electrical boxes and the ship's steering quadrant (lower left) are of great interest to properly trained, experienced scuba divers.* PHOTOS BY JON ZEAMAN.

Wisconsin

(#24 on the map on p. 269)

VESSEL NAME:	WISCONSIN
RIG:	iron steamer
DIMENSIONS:	209' x 40' x 20'9"
LAUNCHED:	Tuesday, October 11, 1881; Wyandotte, MI
DATE LOST:	Tuesday, October 29, 1929
CAUSE OF LOSS:	foundered in a storm
CARGO:	iron castings, automobile parts, oil
LIVES LOST:	9 (from a total of 68 on board)
GENERAL LOCATION:	6.5 miles ESE of Kenosha, Wisconsin
DEPTH:	90' - 130'
ACCESS:	boat
DIVING SKILL LEVEL:	advanced
DIVING HAZARDS:	depth, darkness, penetration, silting, current
CO-ORDINATES:	Lat/Lon: 42.31.80 / 87.42.55
	Loran: 33147.41 / 49634.04

At seven o'clock in the morning of Tuesday, October 29, 1929, the 209' iron passenger and package freighter, *Wisconsin*, foundered several miles off Kenosha, Wisconsin, with the loss of nine lives. The dramatic events leading to this tragic sinking had commenced several hours earlier.

The *Wisconsin* departed Chicago harbor for Milwaukee during a severe storm, with strong northeast winds blowing and waves cresting over the ship's bow. Steel casings broke loose from the cargo and punctured several of the 48-year-old iron hull plates at 1:00 A.M., October 29, 1929. Water quickly flooded the fire holds, extinguishing the ship's power. Captain Douglas H. Morrison radioed for help, indicating his position, the immediacy of the danger, and the fact that his ship was drifting towards Kenosha's shoreline. He then dropped both ship's anchors, immediately stopping his vessel's drift into shallower water and possible safety. At 4:00 A.M., Coast Guard rescue boats at the scene could not budge the anchored, sinking *Wisconsin*. Captain Morrison then realized that, without steam power, he could not raise his anchors! Cool heads had not prevailed. Captain Morrison gave the "Abandon ship!" command. Since the vessel listed heavily to port, the starboard lifeboats could not be launched. The *Wisconsin* then sent its final radio message: "Not enough boats for us all," tragically familiar words.

All of the passengers and most of the crew were removed from the sinking *Wisconsin* by a steel fish tug and the Coast Guard boats. Captain Morrison and eight sailors stayed with the ship, hoping that their running mate, the steamer, *Illinois*, would reach them in time and tow them to Kenosha. Unfortunately, time ran out. The *Wisconsin* sank with the nine men. Captain Morrison was actually yanked from the water alive, but he died later on shore.

The combination passenger and freight steamer, Wisconsin, *was 48 years old when she sank in late 1929 with the loss of nine lives.* GREAT LAKES MARINE COLLECTION OF THE MILWAUKEE PUBLIC LIBRARY/WISCONSIN MARINE HISTORICAL SOCIETY.

The *Wisconsin* packed an adventurous life into her 48 years. Launched as the *Wisconsin* on October 11, 1881, by the Detroit Dry Dock Company at Wyandotte, Michigan, she worked under the banner of Chicago's Goodrich Transit Company from 1881 to 1883, when she was purchased by the Grand Haven & Milwaukee Transportation Company of Milwaukee, who owned her until 1896. During that period, in March of 1885, the *Wisconsin* suffered major hull damage after being trapped in ice off Grand Haven, Michigan, for two weeks. Purchased by the Crosby Transporation Company of Muskegon, Michigan, in 1896, her name was changed to *Naomi* on January 31, 1899. The bad luck superstitiously associated with changing a ship's name hit the ship on May 21, 1907, when she caught fire in mid-lake off Grand Haven. Four lives were lost, and the burned out hulk was towed to Manitowoc for rebuilding. The ship was dropped from enrollment on May 22, 1907, and, after a two-year hiatus, was re-enrolled on March 29, 1909. Rebuilding was completed by early 1910, when the ship's name was changed again (some people never learn) to

E.G. Crosby, on May 18, 1910 (two years later, Mr. E.G. Crosby went down with the *Titanic).* During World War I, the ship was taken over by Uncle Sam, purchased by the United States Shipping Board and renamed the *General Robert M. O'Reilly* for use on the Atlantic Coast as a hospital convalescent ship in New York harbor in 1918. After the war, the vessel was purchased by the Chicago, Racine, & Milwaukee Steamship Company of Milwaukee in November, 1919, and returned to Milwaukee on December 19, 1919. She was then renamed the *Pilgrim.* Not seeing much action with this company, the ship was purchased by her original owner, the Goodrich Transit Company, on June 29, 1922. So popular was the ship at her gala return to the Chicago-Milwaukee run that the company decided to truly come full circle and give the aging vessel back her original name. On August 12, 1924, she was officially renamed the *Wisconsin.* What an incredible odyssey for a ship!

Each of the staterooms, all on the upper level of the iron-hulled steamer, WISCONSIN, *supplied its passengers with running water. This statement is indeed ironic today, in light of the ship's present position.*   PHOTO BY JON ZEAMAN.

The *Wisconsin's* 1920's layout ensured her popularity with passengers. This fast ship was fitted for comfort. Each stateroom, equipped with running water, upper and lower berths, and call bells, was on the outside, ensuring good ventilation and views. The *Wisconsin* ran Lake Michigan year-round. On her last voyage, she carried, among other things in her cargo holds, automobiles, iron castings, prescription whiskey ("prescription" because Prohibition, which outlawed alcohol, was in effect, so alcohol could be procured legally only for medicinal purposes), barrels of brass plumbing fixtures, boxes of brass rivets for horse harnesses, cans of varnish, welding rods, and Christmas toys.

The *Wisconsin* sank early in the morning of Tuesday, October 29, 1929. That day became known in history as "Black Tuesday," not because of the *Wisconsin*, but because something much larger than a ship sank. That afternoon, the stock market crashed dramatically, plunging the world into a serious, ten-year, economic situation we now refer to as the Great Depression.

Chicago diver, Dick Race, located the *Wisconsin* in 1961. This shipwreck lies 6.5 miles ESE of Kenosha, Wisconsin, upright in 130' of water. The ship rises about 40' from the mud and sand lake bottom. More and more of her hull is settling deeply into the soft lake bottom. The port anchor chain winds around the bow and trails off to where her anchor lies firmly embedded in the sand. The superstructure, with its 100 passenger staterooms, is virtually all broken down flat or missing, much of it swept away by natural elements. The smokestack, red paint still visible, lies lengthwise on deck. At the bow in the forward cargo hold, the windlass sits below the capstan on deck. Three vintage 1920's automobiles (a Chevrolet, a Hudson, and an Essex) in an incredible state of preservation grace the rear cargo hold. Radios and a tractor can also be found below deck. Much of the exposed area of the Wisconsin shipwreck suffers from strong currents. For other areas, take along a good dive light (or two or three). Remember what I've been saying about the dangers of penetration diving. Exploring the inside of a shipwreck has all the dangers of cave diving, plus more.

Bitts on the WISCONSIN'S *bow originally provided good anchorage for ropes holding the steamer fast to a dock. Today they make perfectly willing and stationary subjects for underwater photography.* PHOTO BY JON ZEAMAN.

5 Lake Superior Shipwrecks

"Five Great Lakes --- one, Superior."

---popular saying among people who proudly
live along Lake Superior's shoreline.

[Artwork from the *Chicago Inter Ocean,* April 2, 1893]

The awestruck writer of the following account, reprinted with its inherent
spelling errors and geographic inaccuracies in an Upper Canada
newspaper, the *Hallowell Free Press* (Picton, Ontario) on Tuesday,

October 30, 1832, conveyed successfully the enormous size and impressive presence of Lake Superior:

"Lake Superior, without the aid of any great effort of imagination, may be considered as the inexhaustible spring from whence, through unnumbered ages, the St. Lawrence has continued to derive its ample stream. This immense Lake, unequaled in magnitude by any collection of fresh water upon the globe, is situated between the parallels of 56 deg. 25 min. and 49 deg. 1 min. north Latitude, and the meridians of 84 deg. 34 min. and 92 deg. 14 min. west longitude. Its length measured on a curve line through the centre, is about 350 geographical miles, its extreme bredth one hundred and forty, and its circumference, in following the sinuosities of the coast, about one thousand five hundred. Its surface is about six hundred and twenty-seven feet above the tide water of the Atlantic; but the shore exhibits almost conclusive indications of its having been, in former ages as much, perhaps, as 40 or 50 feet above its present level. --- Various soundings have been taken from eighty to one hundred and fifty fathoms, but its greatest depth probably exceeds two hundred fathoms *[author's note: a fathom is six feet]*; thus demonstrating the bottom of the lake to be nearly six hundred feet below the level of the ocean. --- The chrystalline transparency of its waters is unrivalled, and such as to render rocks at an extraordinary depth distinctly vissible [sic]. The bottom of the lake ciefly [sic] consists of a very adhesive clay, which speedily indurates by atmospheric exposure, and contains small shells of the species at present existing in the lake. A sea almost of itself, this lake is subject to many vicissitudes of that element, for here the storm rages and the billows break, with a violence scarcely surpassed by the tempests of the ocean, but is not subject to the oceanic phenomena displayed by an unerring and periodical flux and reflux. Its expansive surface, however, yields to the influence of heavy winds; so that when these blow strong from one quarter they produce a very preceptible [sic] rise of the lake in the opposite direction. The spring freshets are also known to have occasioned a rapid swelling of the waters, which has been especially conspicuous after a rigorous winter. That its waters were once salt is by no means unlikely, and the supposition stands, in some degree supported by the nature of the fish that inhabit them, and the marine shells that are found along the beaches, or are imbedded in the shores."

---from *Bouchette's British Dominion in North America.*

In 1832, maritime traffic on that lake was still limited to canoes and small sailboats; little did that writer realize that, 150 years later, Lake Superior's reputation for towering power and unbridled fury ("here the storm rages and the billows break") could be easily proven by pointing to the hundreds of shipwrecks and sailors' corpses pockmarking the lake's bottom.

Étienne Brûlé, the first European to have seen Lake Huron about a dozen years earlier, was probably, along with fellow explorer Grenoble, the first white man to lose his breath at the sight of Lake Superior in 1622. Later French explorers, Radisson and Groseilliers, traveled extensively by canoe on Lake Superior in 1659-1660 gathering valuable furs, at the same time that French Jesuit missions were being set up to Christianize the natives. One of these missionaries, Claude-Jean Allouez, drifted from his spiritual duties, drawn by the enticingly mysterious and worldly lure of the lake, circumnavigated and charted Lake Superior in 1667. Before losing control of this region to the British in the late 1700's, the French called this massive body of water "le lac supérior," meaning "upper lake," a reference to its position northwest of Lake Huron. Lake Superior remained a completely British region until John Jacob Astor established his American Fur Company at Duluth in 1817.

Here are some quick facts about the lake:

- Lake Superior is bordered on the north and east by the province of Ontario, on the west by the state of Minnesota, and on the south by the states of Michigan and Wisconsin. The international boundary runs for a total distance of 283 miles across the middle region of the lake.

- Lake Superior is approximately 383 miles long (east to west) and 160 miles wide (north to south).

- The deepest spot in this largest of the Great Lakes is 1,333 feet, or about 222 fathoms, discovered only in recent years, about 38 miles north of Munising, Michigan and about 38 miles southeast of Stannard Rock. This profound depth could easily contain the entire 1,250' height of New York City's Empire State Building, even with a 50-foot-tall King Kong perched atop.

- The surface area of Lake Superior covers 11,100 square miles within Canada, and 20,600 square miles within the United States, for an overwhelming total of 31,700 square miles.

- The mean, or average, depth of Lake Superior is 487 feet. There is more water in Lake Superior (2,935 cubic miles) than in the combined volume of all four of the other Great Lakes (which totals 2,538 cubic miles). The water retention (or change-over) time for Lake Superior is between 110 and 190 years, the highest rate for any of the Great Lakes.

- Lake Superior receives most of its water from about 200 rivers that flow into it, and it discharges into Lake Huron at its southeastern end, dropping at the Sault Rapids/St. Mary's River from Lake Superior's mean surface elevation of exactly 600 feet above sea level to Lake Huron's level of 579 feet above the oceans.

- Lake Superior's coastline is rugged, remote, sparsely-settled, and picturesque, indented with deep, blue bays surrounded by high cliffs and sprinkled with rocky shoals and heavily forested islands.

- The valuable mineral deposits around Lake Superior, particularly copper and iron ore, caught the attention of the early French Jesuit explorers and, particularly, nineteenth-century entrepreneurs, who pushed for the completion of the ship canal along the St. Mary's River at Sault Ste. Marie in 1855, connecting Lake Superior commercially with the rest of the Great Lakes system.

- The most isolated lighthouse marks the most dangerous reef in Lake Superior at Stannard Rock. Named after its 1840's discoverer, Capt. Charles Stannard, the light, perched 102 feet above the lake, began operation on July 4, 1882.

- There are several notoriously dangerous shoal areas in remote and distant parts of Lake Superior. Just to the northeast of isolated Stannard Rock, the depth is only seven fathoms, or 42 feet. Superior's storm waves have reached heights in excess of 30 feet, so their troughs in shoal areas could easily lower a freighter enough to hit bottom and sink. Accidentally discovered in 1929 by the *Margaret,* a U.S. Lake Survey ship, Superior Shoal lies halfway between Isle Royale and Michipicoten Island, with a depth of 11 fathoms (66 feet) at its shallowest point. Chummy Bank, about halfway between Michipicoten Island and Caribou Island, bears nine fathoms (53 feet) as its shallowest point, while Southwest Bank, about 12 miles southwest of Caribou Island, shallows to seven fathoms (42 feet). It is near these distant, dangerous shoals that major shipwreck discoveries will be made in the near future.

- The constant low temperatures of Lake Superior's waters prevent decay, so shipwrecks stay the best preserved of all those in the Great Lakes, while the bodies of drowned sailors or passengers sink to the lake's bottom and stay there, frozen for years.

- The first sailing vessel on Lake Superior was a 25-ton ship built at the Sault by French commandant, Louis Denis, Sieur de la Ronde, in 1734; her final disposition is unknown. The North West Company owned a small schooner transporting its furs across Lake Superior as early as 1778. The first recorded shipwreck on the lake was one of that company's schooners, *Invincible,* built in 1802 and wrecked at Whitefish Point on Nov. 14, 1816, with no loss of life.

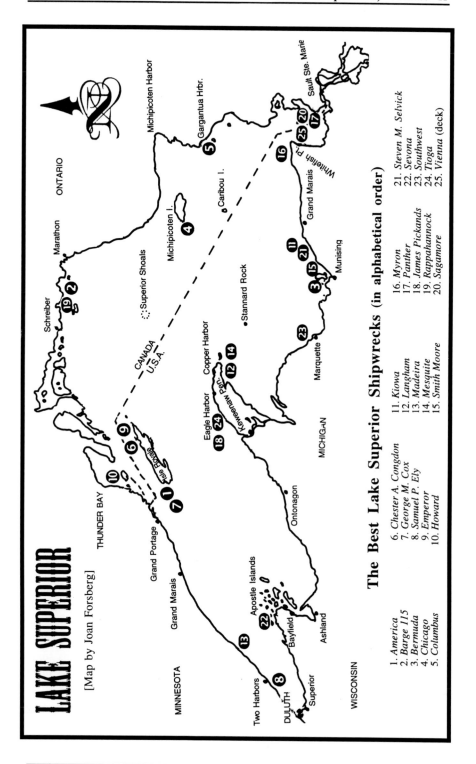

LAKE SUPERIOR

[Map by Joan Forsberg]

The Best Lake Superior Shipwrecks (in alphabetical order)

1. America
2. Barge 115
3. Bermuda
4. Chicago
5. Columbus
6. Chester A. Congdon
7. George M. Cox
8. Samuel P. Ely
9. Emperor
10. Howard
11. Kiowa
12. Langham
13. Madeira
14. Mesquite
15. Smith Moore
16. Myron
17. Panther
18. James Pickands
19. Rappahannock
20. Sagamore
21. Steven M. Selvick
22. Sevona
23. Southwest
24. Tioga
25. Vienna (deck)

- The first steamship on Lake Superior took seven weeks to haul overland around the Sault Rapids in late 1845 and early 1846. This was the 119-foot-long *Independence,* built at Chicago in 1845. Unfortunately, her boiler exploded in Lake Superior just above the Sault Rapids on November 22, 1854, killing four people. Parts of this historic ship, including the unusual propeller on display in the Soo Locks Park in the Michigan Sault, were recovered in 1933.

- The sidewheel steamer, *Superior,* built at Perrysburg, Ohio in 1845, was one of the last ships portaged around the rapids at Sault Ste. Marie and into Lake Superior before the construction of the Sault locks in 1853-55. The 184-foot-long *Superior* was later dashed to pieces near the high cliffs of Pictured Rocks National Seashore east of Munising after losing her rudder on October 30, 1856, resulting in one of the worst loss-of-life wrecks on Lake Superior: about 35 of the 55 people on board perished.

- Lake Superior holds the secrets of the most famous (thanks in large part to a popular, haunting ballad by Canadian folksinger and sailor, Gordon Lightfoot, in 1976) and largest (with a length of 729 feet) shipwreck in the Great Lakes proper, namely the steel freighter, *Edmund Fitzgerald,* which sank in 529 feet of Canadian water off Whitefish Point on November 10, 1975, with the loss of all 29 men on board. No body was ever recovered, a tragic fact converted to poetic personification in the line, "Superior never gives up her dead." The wound of this modern maritime misfortune still aches today, but public fascination with the *Edmund Fitzgerald* has created a legend fueling a mini-industry.

- There are approximately 500 shipwrecks in Lake Superior, most of them as yet undiscovered. Many will never be discovered because they no longer exist, having been dashed to thousands of small pieces along the lake's rocky shoreline.

- The state of Michigan has created Lake Superior underwater preserves at Whitefish Point, Munising (named the Alger County Underwater Preserve), Marquette, and at the Keweenaw Peninsula. Wisconsin has the Apostle Islands National Lakeshore, the waters of which contain several shipwrecks (a required diving permit can be picked up free at the visitor Center in Bayfield and at the Little Sand Bay Visitor Center). Isle Royale National Park contains some of the most fascinating shipwrecks in the lake; scuba divers must register their activities here, also, prior to scuba diving these sites. As with all shipwrecks in the entire Great Lakes system, care should be taken to leave the site as undisturbed as possible. "Take only pictures (and fond memories); leave only bubbles."

America (#1 on the map on p. 355)

VESSEL NAME:	AMERICA
RIG:	passenger steamer
DIMENSIONS:	164' 6" x 31' x 11'
LAUNCHED:	Sat., April 2, 1898; Wyandotte, Michigan
DATE LOST:	Thursday, June 7, 1928
CAUSE OF LOSS:	stranded
CARGO:	passengers
LIVES LOST:	none (one dog)
GENERAL LOCATION:	Washington Harbor, Isle Royale
DEPTH:	4' to 85'
ACCESS:	boat
DIVING SKILL LEVEL:	intermediate-advanced
DIVING HAZARDS:	penetration, hypothermia, entanglement, silt
CO-ORDINATES:	Lat/Lon: 47.53.39 / 89.13.15
	Loran: 46082.2 / 31909.2

Isle Royale is the largest of Lake Superior's islands, measuring about 45 miles in length and averaging 15 miles in width. Located in the northwestern portion of this enormous freshwater lake, about 16 miles off the Minnesota-Ontario shoreline, forest-shrouded Isle Royale, whose mystic beauty prompted its establishment as a U.S. National Park in 1940, has surrendered the locations of about a dozen of her shipwrecks to visiting scuba divers; all but one (the *Kamloops* in 175' to 255') are within sport diving range. There are, however, no airfill stations or diver support services on Isle Royale itself, and noise limitation rules for the use of private compressors are tightening there.

The natural conditions in Lake Superior, the most northern and least polluted of the Great Lakes, have thwarted the spread of zebra mussels, small bivalve invaders from coastal Europe which arrived and surprisingly proliferated in the southern Great Lakes in the past ten years. The shipwrecks in these Lake Superior waters are still free of multilayered, aesthetics-killing coats of mollusks.

The freight and passenger steamer, *America,* is the probable candidate for being the most popular shipwreck in Isle Royale's waters, both when she was actively afloat and in operation, and now that she plays a passive role as a shipwreck site for scuba divers.

Launched as hull number 127 for the Detroit Dry Dock Company at Wyandotte, Michigan, on Saturday, April 2, 1898, the steel-hulled, oak-decked *America* measured 164' 6" in length and 31' in beam, with a gross tonnage of 486.4 tons. Her triple expansion engine, with the U.S. flag appropriately painted on its side, supplied 700 indicated horsepower. In that spring of 1898, the America commenced daily runs between the Lake Michigan ports of Chicago and Michigan City with an impressive top speed of 18 miles an hour. She occasionally freelanced into Lakes Huron and Erie.

America's Lake Michigan career was short-lived when Booth Steamship Line of Duluth, Minnesota, purchased her in early 1902. For the next 26 years, the ship plied the Lake Superior waters as the prime communication and transportation link carrying passengers and freight on the Duluth-to-Port Arthur (Ontario)-to-Isle Royale route. Her speed continued to be a source of pride, particularly when she won a race with the fast Canadian steamer, *Huronic,* in the spring of 1903.

America was often the first vessel out in the spring and the last one to lay up at the end of the navigation season. Lighthouse keepers often returned to the mainland for the winter on board the *America.*

Despite the challenging nature of this dangerous northshore course on her daily runs, often with fog, wind, rain, snow, or ice adding to the constant hazards of rocks and reefs, *America* remained consistently on schedule and suffered only a few incidents in her long career. On May 4, 1902, the steamer suffered serious damage after colliding with the south pier at the Duluth Ship Canal. Five of her staterooms were destroyed by the steamer *Holmes'* anchor in July, 1904. The *America* damaged her rudder shoe on a reef in Tobin Harbor in October, 1908, and she ran aground at Burlington Point in early summer, 1909, resulting in the replacement of her stem and about 40 feet of her keel. She grounded at Victoria Lighthouse off Fort William, Ontario, on April 10, 1910. In May, 1914, *America* ran aground near Two Rivers, Minnesota, severely damaging her hull. On July 21, 1927, miscommunication in *America's* engine room caused her to collide with a tugboat and a dock at Port Arthur, Ontario, before running aground. So many accidents were not considered unusual in light of these dangerous waters and *America's* busy schedule.

America's accidents were counterbalanced by her respected masters. Edward "Indian" Smith received a promotion from first mate to captain of the *America* upon the death of her original Lake Superior captain, Jacob F. Hector, in 1910. Smith retained the former master's warmth with passengers and crew. His reputation for promptness and friendliness continued for the last 18 years of *America's* operation.

The year 1910 also saw the installation of wireless (radio) on board *America,* two years before that invention's well-publicized major role in the rescue of the *Titanic* survivors. In the course of vessel examination which globally followed the *Titanic* disaster, one Great Lakes newspaper observed that the steamer, *America,* was licensed to carry 450 passengers, but had room for only 108 in her lifeboats. Licensing maximums and life-saving minimums were re-evaluated and improved.

SHIP AHOY!   SHIP AHOY!

Tomorrow Afternoon

THE HERALD Will Give Another of Its Delightful 30-MILES-DOWN-THE-LAKE EXCURSIONS on the Swift Running and Palatial—

STEAMER AMERICA

Fare for the

Round Trip

30c

Fare for the

Round Trip

30c

THE MOST DELIGHTFUL, CONVENIENT AND SATISFACTORY EXCURSION EVER DEVISED.

The Steamer America will leave Booth's Dock, foot of Lake Avenue, promptly at 5 p. m.—returning about 9 p. m.

Robinson's Mandolin Orchestra Will be on board and render a program of popular and classical music during the entire trip.

Bring your lunch baskets and enjoy a picnic on board the finest boat on Lake Superior—Excursionists if they so desire can secure lunches on the boat.

GET TICKETS AT HERALD OFFICE.

Don't delay, but secure yours early, as the number to be sold is limited to insure the comfort and pleasure of all who go.

Advertisement for a popular and inexpensive Lake Superior evening excursion on board AMERICA *(complete with orchestra!)* DULUTH EVENING HERALD, *August 13, 1906.*

In 1911, *America's* length was increased by 18 feet to 182' 6", adding 12 staterooms and additional tonnage. Her beam remained the same.

The steel steamer, AMERICA, *spent most of her career plying the waters of northwestern Lake Superior.* GREAT LAKES MARINE COLLECTION OF THE MILWAUKEE PUBLIC LIBRARY/ WISCONSIN MARINE HISTORICAL SOCIETY.

On Wednesday, June 6, 1928, the steamer, *America,* set out on her final voyage. She hopped from port to port between Duluth and Grand Marais, Minnesota, on Lake Superior's north shore, before crossing to the west end of Isle Royale for a late night drop-off of two passengers at Washington Harbor.

America departed Washington Harbor in the middle of the night with 31 crew (including God-fearing stokers and immaculate waiters) and only 16 passengers. Captain Smith turned command over to the new first mate, John Wick, at 2:42 A.M. on Thursday, June 7, 1928. First mate Wick was not particularly familiar with these waters, and within five minutes of taking command, the steamer thudded and scraped over a reef at the mouth of the harbor, holing herself, and proceeded to sink. Captain Smith hastily returned to the bridge, where he ordered *America* to be beached on a nearby gravel stretch. However, another reef along the way locked the steamer in a grounded position about 100' off shore, right at a steep underwater drop-off. *America* was doomed.

In orderly fashion, the entire crew and passengers launched the five lifeboats and rowed back in the early morning darkness half a mile to the dock at Washington Harbor. The only casualty was a dog, a water spaniel, belonging to sixteen-year-old twin brothers, Lyman and Leland Clay, who were among the passengers on board *America* that night. They had tied their pet to the steering post below deck in the stern of the ship, and neither Lyman nor a crewman was able to reach the dog before water filled the stern section and was rising in the parallel walkways running through the ship's length. A 1979 report indicated that the dog's remains were still inside the stern of the *America,* tied to the post.

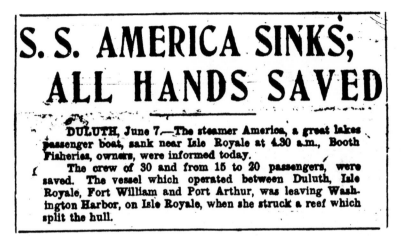

Front-page story in THE DAILY TIMES-JOURNAL *[Fort William, Ontario], June 7, 1928. Only the bare facts were reported at that early time; details were printed the next day.*

"CAPTAIN OF *AMERICA* LAST TO LEAVE," screamed the bold banner headline on the front page of the Fort William, Ontario, *Daily Times-Journal* on June 8, 1928, proclaiming Captain Smith's adherence to that Victorian heroic tradition. However, the main concern of the city's residents was revealed in the slightly smaller headline above the banner: "FRUIT CARGO GOES DOWN WITH VESSEL." Fortunately, the inhabitants of Fort William, Ontario, were not denied the worldly pleasure of their strawberries when the *America* sank, as trucks hastily provided replacements from neighboring areas.

Some initial newspaper accounts incorrectly described the *America* as "lying on the bottom of Lake Superior tonight under 17 fathoms [102'] of water." However, this was not quite the case, and the ship's loss was technically not a sinking, but a stranding, as the vessel's wheelhouse and forward deck remained above the water. Tourists visiting Isle Royale during that summer of 1928 often rowed to the wreck, exploring her visible remains and posing for photographs with the disadvantaged vessel. However, by the spring of 1930, ice, wind, and wave action had torn off the bridge house, with *America's* hull settled just beneath the surface of the water.

Subsequent salvage attempts failed to raise the *America.* Her two anchors, weighing 2,100 and 1,900 pounds, were raised during World War II by the

U.S. Army Corps of Engineers, and the seven-ton smokestack was removed by commercial salvors in 1965.

The AMERICA *sank after hitting a rocky reef in a late-night attempt to cruise out of a wilderness harbor.* GREAT LAKES MARINE COLLECTION OF THE MILWAUKEE PUBLIC LIBRARY/ WISCONSIN MARINE HISTORICAL SOCIETY.

Only 28 years after the *America* sank, the first reports of sport scuba divers visiting the site appeared in the summer of 1956. The group was aptly named the "Frigid Frogs." Dishes were still stacked on the sideboards below deck, and tables were piled high at the lower end of the dining room. One diver later found, in an old desk below deck, legible photographs depicting Chicago's waterfront. Souvenirs removed by 1957 included a bottle of "ripe" meat sauce and the horn from the model T Ford truck that was on board. Sadly, by 1974, the old vehicle's tires and most of its engine parts had been removed by scuba divers thoughtlessly removing "souvenirs" or "tokens of accomplishment." Today, what little remains of this antique vehicle is hardly recognizable. By 1980, most divers living in the Isle Royale area "had at least one piece of the *America* sitting in their garage or basement," according to one longtime, local diver.

A mainland diver asked us to return a number of plates, cups, and other dishware to the *America* when we made a week-long trip there in the late 1980's. This diver, who requested anonymity then and now, realized the immense loss of the significance of these artifacts when they were removed from their historic setting. For years, they had sat in his garage, collecting dust. We handed these

America Shipwreck Site Map

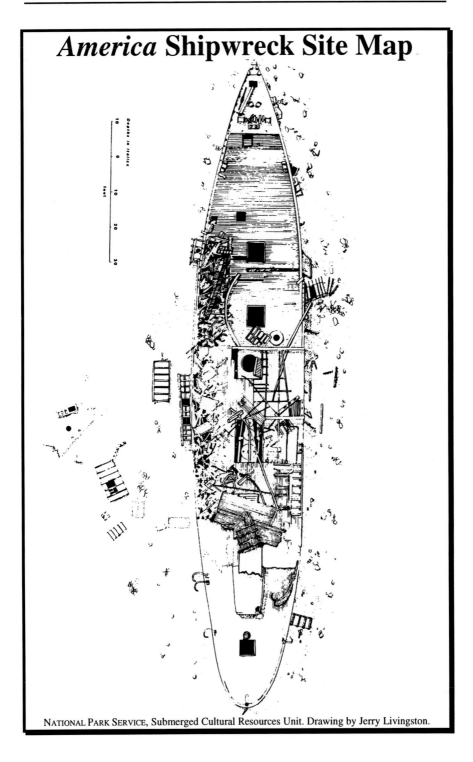

NATIONAL PARK SERVICE, Submerged Cultural Resources Unit. Drawing by Jerry Livingston.

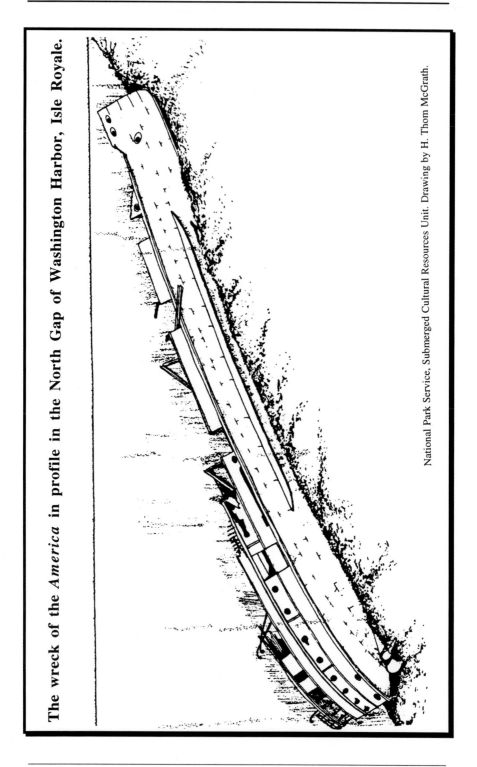

The wreck of the *America* in profile in the North Gap of Washington Harbor, Isle Royale.

National Park Service, Submerged Cultural Resources Unit. Drawing by H. Thom McGrath.

shipwreck goods over to the Isle Royale Park Service, who gratefully put them on exhibit at Port Washington (Windigo) Harbor for all visitors to the island to see and appreciate. Hopefully, in the future, more of *America's* artifacts that today resemble disoriented junk in somebody's basement or attic will be returned to the place where they have much greater importance.

The wreck of the *America* rests in two to 85 feet of clear, cold Lake Superior water on a 45-degree angle on the incline and a 30-degree list to port. Narrow passageways into the wreck offer access to the galley, the dining salon, various staterooms with below-deck corridors aplenty, and the engine room. The pride of *America's* crew is still clearly evident at the place where they painted the American flag onto the side of the engine years ago.

Care must be taken not to become entangled in wiring, plumbing, or other debris, and not to disturb the delicate and vision-obliterating silt. Penetration diving remains the realm of the specially trained and the properly prepared. At the stern, the deepest part of the wreck, the propeller and taffrail are of interest to visiting scuba divers.

The popular *America* shipwreck site can be visited by diver-supplied private boat from the mainland, or by chartering with a scuba dive shop in Grand Portage, Minnesota, or Thunder Bay, Ontario.

A passenger and freight ship from the mainland approaches the Isle Royale site of the sunken steamer, AMERICA, *marked by a white buoy.*   PHOTO BY CRIS KOHL.

ABOVE: *In midship, much of the* AMERICA'S *superstructure has collapsed in disarray. Many planks and pipes crisscross the area and make entry into the shipwreck challenging.* BELOW: *The* AMERICA *offers several hatches and stairwells for exploration below deck by properly trained technical divers.* PHOTOS BY CRIS KOHL.

Visiting scuba divers appreciate a shipwreck that still looks like a ship! The well-defined steel bow of the steamer, AMERICA, *rising to within 4' of the surface, is one of the first dramatic, visual delights experienced at this site.* PHOTO BY CRIS KOHL.

ABOVE: *Another of the many impressive sights on the wreck of the* AMERICA *is the huge triple expansion engine, built by the Dry Dock Engine Works in Detroit, Michigan, in 1898, and capable of producing 700 horsepower.* PHOTO BY CRIS KOHL. BELOW: *Below deck in* AMERICA'S *engine room, divers must be careful not to disturb the fine painting of an American flag on the engine.* PHOTO BY JOYCE HAYWARD.

Barge 115

(#2 on the map on p. 355)

VESSEL NAME:	BARGE 115
RIG:	whaleback
DIMENSIONS:	256' x 36' 1" x 18' 9"
LAUNCHED:	Sat., August 15, 1891; Superior, Wisconsin
DATE LOST:	Monday, December 18, 1899
CAUSE OF LOSS:	stranded
CARGO:	iron ore
LIVES LOST:	none (from 8 on board)
GENERAL LOCATION:	west side of Pic Island, N Lake Superior
DEPTH:	40' - 80'
ACCESS:	boat to the island; from shore there
DIVING SKILL LEVEL:	intermediate
DIVING HAZARDS:	depth, remoteness, hypothermia, silting
CO-ORDINATES:	Lat/Lon:
	Loran:

Whaleback *Barge 115*, the last Great Lakes shipwreck of the 1800's, disappeared somewhere in northern Lake Superior when people on land were busy making preparations for Christmas, which was just a few days away. Regular shore folks did their Christmas shopping while eight sailors fought for their lives in mid-December on the harshest of the Great Lakes.

Captain Alexander McDougall, famed designer and builder of the distinctive steel whalebacks, cigar-shaped, semi-submarine vessels with a bow, or nose, so blunt that they were nicknamed "pigboats," was a practical man who named most of his ships after their hull number. Whaleback *Barge 115* was hull number 15 that his firm, the American Steel Barge Company of West Superior, Wisconsin, had built. The 256' barge, official number 53268, came out as a propulsionless barge in 1891 and remained that way for her eight years of life.

At Two Rivers, Minnesota, the 1,169-gross-ton *Barge 115* was loaded with 3,000 tons of iron ore, attached to the whaleback steamer, *Colgate Hoyt*, and the two headed for the Soo on Dec. 10, 1899, on this final run of the season.

They sailed right into one of the worst storms of the year. Three days later, the ships were only off Pic Island, Ontario, when the tow line parted from the storm strain. The *Hoyt* lost its helpless *Barge 115* and its eight crew.

The frantic *Hoyt* zigzagged back and forth searching for its lost partner, but *Barge 115* was gone. There was nothing to do but to steam to Sault Ste. Marie and find tugs to help scour the lake. This was done, but also to no avail. Lake men feared that *Barge 115* had gone down and its crew were drowned.

Captain Arthur A. Boyce and his seven men were only lost, not dead, but they did drift helplessly in the blizzard for five terrifying days before *barge 115* stranded just off a shore. A small life raft took them all safely to land in shifts. The next day, they began walking along the shoreline amidst thick snow and precipitous cliffs. Before long, they realized that they were on an island.

At an abandoned log cabin, they found spikes, nails, and enough wood to fashion a large raft (since they had left their small raft on the other side of the island) which, by some miracle with all eight men often in water up to their knees, conveyed them to the mainland with their makeshift paddles. Once across, they soon stumbled upon the Canadian Pacific Railroad track and staggered to the nearest town, Middleton, Ontario, more dead than alive. But they were all alive. The first search for missing whaleback *Barge 115* was over.

You will need a boat to take you out to Pic Island, a few miles off Neys Provincial Park on the Canadian mainland. The broken steel remains of this whaleback, located by Ryan LeBlanc in 1980 after the second major search for *Barge 115*, lie on a rock bottom 40' to 80' deep. Only the bow with its deck house is intact, with braided steel wire wrapped around a large windlass. Immense twisted steel sheets, all that remain of the hull, lie scattered nearby.

The crew of the whaleback *Barge 115* lost their ship and cargo, but their lives were saved. All of them made it home just in time to be with their overjoyed families for Christmas, 1899, the last holiday of the nineteenth century, and for New Year's Day, the first day, the dawn, of a new era.

Whaleback BARGE 115 *was destined to be the last Great Lakes shipwreck of that century.* GREAT LAKES MARINE COLLECTION OF THE MILWAUKEE PUBLIC LIBRARY/WISCONSIN MARINE HISTORICAL SOCIETY.

This drawing of the whaleback BARGE 115 *appeared in the* DULUTH NEWS TRIBUNE *on October 27, 1895, more than four years before the vessel's demise. The ship had had a close call in a collision with another whaleback, the* A.D. THOMSON, *off Two Harbors. The journalist argued in favor of the whaleback design: "...One of the most notable examples of the unsinkable qualities of these vessels...." Unfortunately, history proved that writer wrong; over half a dozen whalebacks lie sunk in the Great Lakes.*

A very small cove on the southwest side of Pic Island offers small boat sanctuary at the rocky site of the wrecked whaleback BARGE 115. PHOTO BY CRIS KOHL.

Rusty bits and pieces of the steel whaleback BARGE 115 *ended up a fair distance inland on Pic Island due to the powerful forces of nature.*   PHOTO BY CRIS KOHL.

Bermuda   (#3 on the map on p. 355)

VESSEL NAME:	BERMUDA
RIG:	two-masted schooner
DIMENSIONS:	136' x 26' x 11' 9"
LAUNCHED:	April, 1860; Oswego, New York
DATE LOST:	Sat., October 15, 1870 and October, 1883
CAUSE OF LOSS:	stranded, salvaged, abandoned
CARGO:	iron ore
LIVES LOST:	3 in 1870; none in 1883
GENERAL LOCATION:	Murray Bay, S Grand I., off Munising, MI
DEPTH:	12' - 30'
ACCESS:	boat
DIVING SKILL LEVEL:	all levels can have fun here
DIVING HAZARDS:	silting, penetration, tourist boating traffic
CO-ORDINATES:	Lat/Lon: 46.27.89 / 86.38.81
	Loran: 31647.8 / 47431.2

The upright, intact remains of this mid-1800's canal schooner lying in 30' of water and rising to within 12' of the surface in Murray Bay on the south side of Grand Island just off Munising, Michigan, are so well-preserved that it takes little imagination to picture nineteenth century sailors striding across the deck planks or many miles of Great Lakes water splashing off this speedy bow.

To say that we were impressed when we first explored this wreck in the mid-1980's would be an insulting understatement. This shipwreck is incredibly interesting, explorable above, aside, and below deck from bow to stern, and were it not for the fact that you need a boat to take you to it, this vessel would likely be the most visited shipwreck in the Great Lakes.

Built at Oswego, NY, in 1860 by George Goble, this twin-masted, 136' schooner, official #2160, regularly sailed the great distance across the Great Lakes from Lake Ontario to Lake Superior carrying grain and, later, iron ore. Stranded just east of Marquette, Michigan, in late 1869, the *Bermuda* was recovered and repaired at Detroit in the summer of 1870. With 488 tons of iron ore in her holds, the *Bermuda* stranded in Munising Bay on October 15, 1870, with three lives lost. The ship was stripped of anything useful and abandoned.

Thirteen years later, in October, 1883, the captain of the wrecking tug, *Kate Williams*, succeeded in raising the *Bermuda* and towing her to Grand

Island's Murray Bay, where her lifting chains slipped and she dropped to the location which she presently occupies. About 120 tons of iron ore were recovered then, with smaller subsequent cargo salvages.

The *Bermuda's* deck is enclosed by wooden rails running along most of the vessel's perimeter. Her masts, spars, and rigging are gone, but the foremast hole is quite evident, and the mainmast's location, stepped where some decking is now missing, is revealed by the shroud chainplate locations on the rails. Three hatches on deck lead divers into the hull, which can easily and safely be explored the entire length of the ship. Be sure to take a good look at the centerboard box below deck, as well as samples of the specular iron ore cargo. At the stern, the rudder stock pokes up through the deck.

The *Bermuda*, situated 100 miles west of Sault Ste. Marie, lies within Michigan's Alger Underwater Preserve. It is one of the best lakes' schooners.

The schooner, BERMUDA, *resembled the* OLIVER MITCHELL *(140' x 26' x 13'), shown above, which was built in 1874 at Algonac, Michigan, and sank in the Atlantic Ocean off Long Island in a collision in 1911.* GREAT LAKES MARINE COLLECTION OF THE MILWAUKEE PUBLIC LIBRARY/WISCONSIN MARINE HISTORICAL SOCIETY.

The schooner, BERMUDA'S, *stern offers visiting divers a view of the protruding rudder stock, capped with a standard iron crosshead for the ship's steering mechanism. The depth here is only about 14'.* PHOTO BY CRIS KOHL.

Along the starboard railing near midship, visitors to the BERMUDA *shipwreck can appreciate, thanks to sloppy salvaging, samples of the specular (high grade) iron ore cargo which the ship carried on her last voyage in 1870.* PHOTO BY CRIS KOHL.

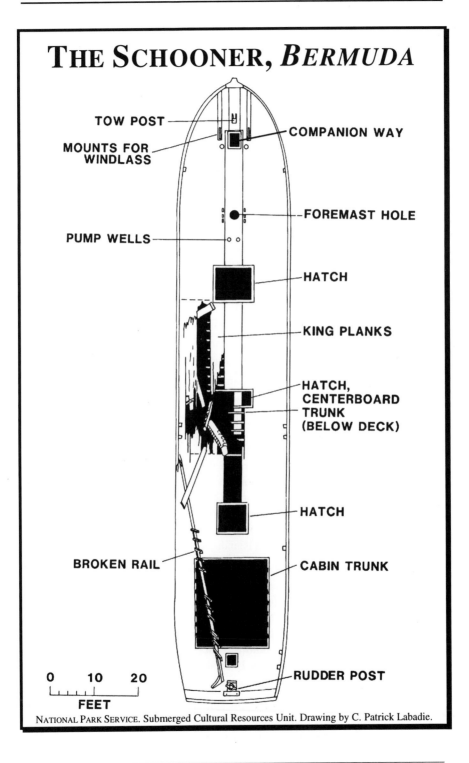

THE SCHOONER, *BERMUDA*

TOW POST

MOUNTS FOR
WINDLASS

COMPANION WAY

FOREMAST HOLE

PUMP WELLS

HATCH

KING PLANKS

HATCH,
CENTERBOARD
TRUNK
(BELOW DECK)

HATCH

BROKEN RAIL

CABIN TRUNK

0   10   20

FEET

RUDDER POST

NATIONAL PARK SERVICE. Submerged Cultural Resources Unit. Drawing by C. Patrick Labadie.

Chicago

(#4 on the map on p. 355)

VESSEL NAME:	CHICAGO
RIG:	steel package freighter (steamer)
DIMENSIONS:	324' 2" x 44' x 14'
LAUNCHED:	Saturday, September 28, 1901; Buffalo, NY
DATE LOST:	Wednesday, October 23, 1929
CAUSE OF LOSS:	stranded; thwarted salvage
CARGO:	zinc ingots and steel fence posts
LIVES LOST:	none (from 31 on board)
GENERAL LOCATION:	Shafer Bay, W. Michipicoten Island, Ont.
DEPTH:	10' - 70'
ACCESS:	boat
DIVING SKILL LEVEL:	intermediate-advanced
DIVING HAZARDS:	remoteness, depth, hypothermia
CO-ORDINATES:	Lat/Lon: 47.43.84 / 85.57.91
	Loran:

At one of the most remote locations in all of the Great Lakes, the wreck of the 324' steel steamer, *Chicago,* lies in 10' to 70' of water. That location is Shafer Bay, at the extreme western end of Michipicoten Island. This massive land entity, third in size after Isle Royale and St. Ignace Island among all of the Lake Superior islands, sits about 35 miles from the nearest mainland marina at Michipicoten Harbor, Ontario. On Michipicoten Island, a handful of commercial fishermen make Quebec Harbor their temporary summer season residence. There are no stores, accommodations, restaurants, marinas, or airfill stations anywhere on this wilderness island.

The 3,195-ton *Chicago,* built at Buffalo, New York, in 1901, succumbed to the rocky reefs at the western end of Michipicoten Island on October 23, 1929, during a blinding snowstorm. No lives were lost from the 31 people who were on board at the time. They camped on the island after removing provisions from their damaged ship. Days later, Coast Guard Cutter No. 119 removed the crew to the tug, *Seminole,* which transported them to Sault Ste. Marie. During salvage operations on December 19, 1929, the ship slid off the rocks and right down a submerged slope, making her a permanent island feature.

This shipwreck lies on her port side in 5' to 70' of water and offers good visibility and views of a capstan on the stern deck, the cargo of zinc ingots, two chains running down a stern hawsepipe, a chain locker, a propeller with a hub, and a stream anchor. The bow in the shallows is badly broken up, but still exhibits a windlass and a popped-out hawsepipe with chain still running through the opening. If you come this far, you will definitely take a good look.

ABOVE: *The huge, steel steamer,* CHICAGO, *toiled on the Great Lakes for 28 years.* GREAT LAKES MARINE COLLECTION OF THE MILWAUKEE PUBLIC LIBRARY/WISCONSIN MARINE HISTORICAL SOCIETY. BELOW: *The* CHICAGO *lay stranded along Michipicoten Island's rocky western edge for two months before sliding down an underwater slope to a permanent rest.* GREAT LAKES HISTORICAL SOCIETY, VERMILION, OHIO.

Columbus

(#5 on the map on p. 355)

VESSEL NAME:	COLUMBUS; launched as JOHN OWEN
RIG:	wooden tug
DIMENSIONS:	136' 2" x 25' 2" x 11' 8"
LAUNCHED:	Saturday, March 7, 1874; Detroit, Michigan
DATE LOST:	Friday, September 10, 1909
CAUSE OF LOSS:	burned
CARGO:	general
LIVES LOST:	none
GENERAL LOCATION:	Gargantua Harbor, Ontario, e. Lake Superior
DEPTH:	0' - 27'
ACCESS:	shore or boat
DIVING SKILL LEVEL:	novice
DIVING HAZARDS:	minimal; remoteness
CO-ORDINATES:	Lat/Lon: wreck visible above water
	Loran: wreck can be seen from shore

Mention Lake Superior shipwrecks to a Great Lakes scuba diver and s/he will likely immediately conjure up images of the elite wrecks in big-name places such as Isle Royale, Whitefish Point, Munising, and Keweenaw. However, not all of the best shipwrecks in this lake are found in those famous areas.

Little-known Gargantua Harbor, remotely nestled on the province of Ontario's eastern Lake Superior shoreline, is a glistening wilderness gem, well worth the one hour it takes to drive the nine miles from the Trans-Canada Highway west along a winding, pot-holed dirt road interrupted periodically by rickety Bailey bridges spanning fast-moving streams.

"If you make it there, you'll join the ranks of a handful of divers who have explored the wreck of the *Columbus*," we were told back in the 1980's by a toughened, northern Ontario diver who was sharing one of the North's best-kept secrets with us.

My adventurous travel companions, Joyce Hayward, with all due respect the queen bee of scuba diving activities in the state of Ohio, and Gary Gentile, energetic Philadelphia deep-diver, underwater photographer, and professional writer, remained undaunted as the road into the bush gradually disappeared altogether. We temporarily abandoned our vehicles at a large, open area within very close range of Lake Superior's icy, blue waters.

The rough road to Garganiua Harbor from the Trans-Canada Highway is nine miles long, and crosses several rickety Bailey bridges, well off the beaten path of the paved highway. This trip, however, is well worth it!   PHOTO BY CRIS KOHL.

It is about a two-mile hike with one's scuba gear and underwater photo equipment carried as best as possible along a relatively level path which runs through the thick northern Ontario wilderness. The nearest boat launch ramp is over 20 miles away, so this harbor sees only the occasional visiting yachtsperson. An inflatable boat, however, can be carried over the stony beach from the vehicle parking lot and launched, saving a long and, sometimes, depending upon the weather and the amount of equipment being transported, arduous hike to Gargantua Harbor.

Not having an inflatable boat with us on our first visit to this site, we had to hike with our gear. Gary had found a long, thick branch which he now yoked over the back of his neck and shoulders, carefully balancing his heavy weightbelt on one end counterbalanced by his drysuit and other equipment in a bag on the other end. The scuba tank, with regulator attached, was carried like a knapsack. It was the only time I ever saw Gary dive with a single tank!

Joyce and I trudged along, lugging our gear in similar makeshift fashion. It happened to be the hottest day in August, and I quickly realized that attempting to wear my full wetsuit while engaged in cattle-like labor over long distance lacked comfort. Fortunately, our lowland trail followed the Lake Superior shoreline, so refreshing water for a quick dip was never far away. Unfortunately, northern Canadian woods near water also breed gigantic mosquitoes.

Gargantua Harbor must be one of the prettiest natural bays ever created, with its long, curving swath of sandy beach at the end of the rounded harbor, and the very gradual deepening of its crystalline water to the sudden drop-off point. An azure sky of deepest summer crowned this perfect setting that day. The relaxing serenity of this place belied its bustling activities of the past.

At the turn of the century, commercial fishing and some tourism created the community of Gargantua Harbor. Catches of herring and lake trout were iced and packed there. By the 1950's, however, the sea lamprey had devastated commercial fishing, and, although lamprey control measures have helped revive fish populations, the community at Gargantua Harbor has remained a ghost town. Two people apparently linger as the sole residents of this site; their appearance, however, is as elusive as their existence is questionable.

A couple of abandoned buildings and the foundations of several others are all that remain to be seen of civilization above water at Gargantua Harbor. The underwater world, however, shelters items of even greater interest.

The huge tug, COLUMBUS, *burned to a total loss in 1909 at Gargantua Harbor.* INSTITUTE FOR GREAT LAKES RESEARCH, BOWLING GREEN STATE UNIVERSITY, OHIO.

The main historic attraction at this backwoods harbor site is the wreck of the large, wooden tug, *Columbus.* The top of the steam engine protrudes above the water, making the vessel's remains easy to locate near the north shore opposite the abandoned fishing sheds. Gazing at the exposed metalwork, one realizes that something big happened here a long time ago.

Launched as the *John Owen* on March 7, 1874 by the Detroit Dry Dock Company, the 328-ton ship measured 136' 2" in length, 25' 2" in beam, and 11' 8" in draft. She was the largest of the early Detroit River tugs. According to the *Inland Lloyds,* the *John Owen* was valued at $36,000 in 1875 when the ship was quite new. In 1882, when J. Emory Owen, among others, of Detroit owned this tug, her value was $25,000; F. W. Gilchrist of Alpena, Michigan, owned the ship in 1893, when her value had remained consistently the same over the past nine years. Grummond of Detroit owned the *John Owen* and used her as a wrecker in 1894, when his vessel was valued at $20,000. The tug was rebuilt in 1898, but the value of this 30-year-old ship by 1906 was only $15,000.

Sold in 1907 to a Canadian named Joseph Ganley of Sault Ste. Marie, Ontario, who changed her name to *Columbus* (her official U.S. number, 75608, was changed to official Canadian number 117039), the vessel spent three seasons transporting supplies to Canadian backports on Lake Superior until, on September 10, 1909, she caught fire while at dock at Gargantua Harbor and was cut loose to prevent the destruction of the pier. She sank in the harbor.

Be prepared to hike a couple of miles with your scuba gear to Gargantua Harbor from the point where you have to leave your vehicle. It is easier to take along an inflatable boat and carry it the short distance to the stony beach. PHOTO BY CRIS KOHL.

The ship's deck and superstructure were destroyed by the flames, but the hull and machinery offer visiting scuba divers ample opportunities for casual explorations or detailed examinations. The *Columbus,* which now lies on her port side, had her bow sheathed for light ice work. Among the interesting items in the debris are a capstan (used to haul up the anchor), innumerable spikes, and a large, four-bladed propeller. The boiler is still very photogenic, although it has toppled over from its firebed. The remains of the *Columbus* rest on a sandy bottom, thinly but evenly punctuated by long-grassed aquatic growth, in a maximum of 30' of clear, Lake Superior water.

Along the shore opposite the *Columbus* site are half a dozen submerged cribs, or log frameworks filled with large rocks and utilized as a stable base for the community's dock. Fishing community cast-offs from the past hundred years clutter the bottom near the cribs. Sunken logs and submerged trees mingle with manmade machine parts and domestic items such as tea kettles.

At the end of the line of cribs, in shallow water ranging from four to 25 feet in depth, lies an abandoned flatbed workbarge with huge cleats and a distinctive winch mounted on the deeper stern end. It takes little imagination to envision the amount of labor, years ago, that this vital workhorse supplied for the community.

Since this site is so remote, plan your dive well and allot your air supply wisely to ensure that you can investigate everything you want to see. Unless you bring your own compressor, the nearest airfill station is near Sault Ste. Marie, Ontario, about 60 miles away. If you hike in with your scuba gear, avoid over-exertion or overheating.

Exploring the underwater portions of this area, as well as drinking in the natural beauty of topside Gargantua Harbor, should imbue anyone with wonder, respect and tranquility. Remember that, since this area is within the boundaries of Lake Superior Provincial Park, it is highly illegal to disturb anything in nature, including the shipwreck in the bay. Please leave all items just as you found them so that future divers visiting this site may also be enriched by the totality of what they see and feel here.

The COLUMBUS' *engine rises to the surface.* PHOTO BY CRIS KOHL.

ABOVE: *The fishing community of Gargantua Harbor was once thriving with activity. Today, only one of the several buildings is still in use. A dock once sat on these submerged cribs just off shore.* BELOW: *Although the wooden steam tug,* COLUMBUS, *was considerably destroyed by fire almost a century ago, many portions of this wreck, such as the bow area, are incredibly interesting.* PHOTO BY CRIS KOHL.

Approaching one of the large propeller blades, diver Gary Gentile explores the remains of the steamer, COLUMBUS', *stern area.* PHOTO BY CRIS KOHL.

Diver Joyce Hayward poses with the charred, but highly interesting and photogenic, remains of the huge tugboat, COLUMBUS. PHOTO BY CRIS KOHL.

Congdon, Chester A. (bow)

(#6 on the map on p. 355)

VESSEL NAME:	CHESTER A. CONGDON; launched as the SALT LAKE CITY
RIG:	steel freighter
DIMENSIONS:	532' x 56' 2" x 26' 5"
LAUNCHED:	Thursday, August 29, 1907; S. Chicago, IL
DATE LOST:	Wednesday, November 6, 1918
CAUSE OF LOSS:	stranded, broke in two
CARGO:	wheat
LIVES LOST:	none (from 37 on board)
GENERAL LOCATION:	Canoe Rocks, northeastern Isle Royale
DEPTH:	70' - 111'
ACCESS:	boat
DIVING SKILL LEVEL:	advanced
DIVING HAZARDS:	depth, hypothermia, darkness, penetration
CO-ORDINATES:	Lat/Lon: 48.11.37 / 88.30.51
	Loran: 46147.8 / 31717.5

The 532' steamer, *Chester A. Congdon*, lost with her 390,154 bushels of wheat at Isle Royale in 1918, became the Great Lakes' largest shipwreck to date and their first million dollar shipping loss. The vessel is also Isle Royale's largest shipwreck, nosing out the steel steamer, *Emperor* (see pp. 401-405) by seven feet in length, although the *Emperor's* gross tonnage exceeds the *Congdon's* by a good 500 tons.

The horrors of the four-year-long international conflict known as World War I were only five days away from officially ending when the *Chester A. Congdon* became a serious shipping casualty. The steel bulk freighter departed Fort William, Ontario, in the middle of the night, at 2:28 A.M., November 6, 1918. Once her nose extended beyond the protected bay waters, the vessel encountered heavy seas and strong gales which prompted her to run back a few miles at 4:00 A.M. and drop anchor. By the time the ship left again and passed Thunder Cape at 10:40 A.M., a heavy fog had set in. Captain Charles J. Autterson decided to make a blind run at nine miles an hour for two and a half hours on a course for Passage Island, where he would drop anchor again and wait for better conditions if the fog persisted.

The CHESTER A. CONGDON, *launched as the* SALT LAKE CITY *in 1907, was renamed in 1912 after a Duluth business friend of the owner.*   AUTHOR'S COLLECTION.

Unfortunately, the *Congdon* sailed slightly off course, but this minute variation was enough to ground the vessel, suddenly, unexpectedly, and violently, on the southerly reef of Canoe Rocks off the northeast side of Isle Royale. A curious fishing launch approached the stranded steamer with an offer of assistance, and it took the *Congdon's* second mate to Port Arthur, Ontario, on the mainland to fetch wrecking assistance. A vessel immediately removed the *Congdon's* crew and carried them to safety. A tug and a barge quickly arrived at the site and removed about 30,000 bushels of wheat from the *Congdon's* forward hold before 55-mile-per-hour winds forced them to seek shelter on November 8th. By the time they returned two days later, the *Congdon's* back was broken. Another 50,000 bushels of wheat were salvaged before the ship and the remainder of her cargo were declared a total loss by the underwriters.

James Playfair, a Midland, Ontario, entrepreneur, paid $10,000 for the rights to the impaled *Chester A. Congdon*, planning to make a successful and financially rewarding salvage. But the gambler, Playfair, played a bad hand. By the spring of 1919 when salvage could finally be undertaken, not a stick nor a kernel of the ship and her cargo could be seen. Her two halves had broken apart and slid down either side of the shoal into deep water. Today that reef is named Congdon Shoal.

Launched as the *Salt Lake City* on August 29, 1907, at South Chicago, Illinois by the Chicago Ship Building Company, the enormous, 532', 6,530-gross-ton, steel ship was renamed *Chester A. Congdon* (after Chester Adgate

Congdon, a Duluth lawyer and mining company director who lived from 1853 to 1916) on February 2, 1912, when she joined the Tomlinson fleet. She was powered by a triple expansion steam engine capable of providing 1,765 indicated horsepower, and her two Scotch induced draft type boilers each measured 14' 6" x 11' 6". Her official number was 204526. At the time of loss, the vessel was owned by the Continental Steamship Company of Duluth, Minnesota, managed by G.A. Tomlinson.

The steel steamer, CHESTER A. CONGDON, *became the largest shipwreck and the first million dollar shipping loss in the entire Great Lakes when the vessel stranded and broke up at Isle Royale in 1918.* REV. PETER VAN DER LINDEN COLLECTION.

This enormous shipwreck cannot be explored on a single scuba dive, the obvious reason being that the two halves are a fair distance apart and at different depths on opposite sides of the rocky reef which rises to within ten feet of the surface. The bow half of the *Chester A. Congdon*, sitting upright on the angle of Congdon Shoal's slope, is usually buoyed by Isle Royale National Park personnel. The pilot house is intact on the bow, which rests in 110' of water and rises to about 70', or 60' if you include the forward mast. The windlass on the bow was salvaged, and the rectangular hole just below the chain locker appears more like a hatch. Four doors provide access into the bow cabins just below the small pilot house. The stern half, with the engine room and stern cabins lying deepest, sit on a dangerously steep incline in 50' to 200' of water on the other side of Congdon Shoal, and is not normally buoyed because the excessive depth and usually poor visibility makes it a dangerous dive. Broken pieces of the *Congdon's* steel hull lie scattered at the top of the shoal in ten feet of water.

THE BOW OF THE STEAMER,
CHESTER A. CONGDON

NATIONAL PARK SERVICE. Submerged Cultural Resources Unit. Drawing by Jerry Livingston.

Cox, George M.(#7 on the map on p. 355)

VESSEL NAME:	GEORGE M. COX; launched as PURITAN
RIG:	passenger steamer
DIMENSIONS:	259' x 40' 5" x 26' 6"
LAUNCHED:	Wednesday, May 1, 1901; Toledo, Ohio
DATE LOST:	Saturday, May 27, 1933
CAUSE OF LOSS:	stranded
CARGO:	passengers
LIVES LOST:	none (from 121 on board)
GENERAL LOCATION:	Rock Island Reef, w. Isle Royale, Michigan
DEPTH:	12' - 97'
ACCESS:	boat
DIVING SKILL LEVEL:	intermediate-advanced
DIVING HAZARDS:	hypothermia, depth, disorientation
CO-ORDINATES:	Lat/Lon: 47.51.56 / 89.19.52
	Loran: 31934.9 / 46069.8

The *George M. Cox* became the most dramatic looking shipwreck at Isle Royale, as well as initiating Lake Superior's largest mass maritime rescue – both occurring on the ship's maiden voyage under her new name and new owner!

The newly-refurbished (at a cost of $80,000) *George M. Cox*, radiant from a freshly-dried coat of glistening white marine paint, virtually flew at 17 knots over the cold waters of Lake Superior, running from Houghton, Michigan, on the Keweenaw Peninsula, towards Port Arthur, Ontario, 90 miles away. The ship had departed Chicago just three days earlier on her maiden voyage in her new condition, carrying 32 distinguished guests who were served by a crew of 89. Descriptions of such lavish living undoubtedly raised the hopes of more than a few ordinary people in 1933, one of the worst years of the Great Depression. At Port Arthur, the *Cox* would be boarded to full capacity (she could accommodate 400 passengers) who would be conveyed in first-class quarters to Chicago for the Century of Progress World's Fair Exposition of 1933.

Mr. George M. Cox, the proud, confident financial wizard and king of the Duke Transportation Company, had purchased the ship, then named the *Puritan,* in late 1932, and named it after himself. He also announced his formation of the Isle Royale Transportation Line, of which the *Cox* would be the first luxurious ship in his fleet. Publicity stops with ship's tours at Manistee and Hancock enticed hundreds of people who generated much acclaim.

Now, as the *Cox* sped towards Canada, both the ship and a fog blanket approached Isle Royale. The vessel did not slow down once the fog embraced her. At full speed, the *Cox* crossed the unseen granite ridge until the rock rose suddenly to within four feet of the surface. The sudden impact tore the four boilers below deck from their mounting cradles, while the hard rock peeled open the steel hull like an automatic can opener for a distance of about 100'. It was 6:20 P.M., and the guests, all at dinner, sprawled forward with their chairs in chaotic unison with the fine china, exquisite crystal, and gourmet cuisine which slid from the tables. Below deck, tools and oil barrels battered the surprised crew. The ship's bow was completely out of the water, pointing towards heaven. An S.O.S. was immediately transmitted. Lifeboats were launched, filled, and headed to the lighthouse a mile away, its foghorn now audible to all.

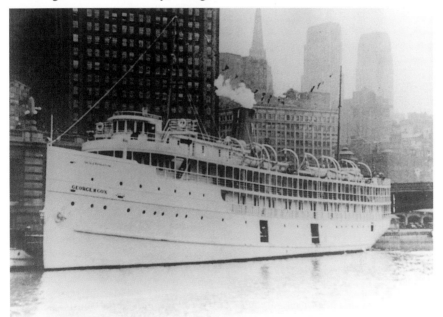

Launched as the PURITAN *in 1901, George M. Cox named the ship after himself when he purchased it for his transportation company.* GREAT LAKES MARINE COLLECTION OF THE MILWAUKEE PUBLIC LIBRARY/WISCONSIN MARINE HISTORICAL SOCIETY.

First mate Arthur J. Cronk, who had been first mate when the steamer, *Kiowa*, wrecked on Lake Superior four years earlier, and who had to take command of that sinking ship after his captain drowned when his lifeboat capsized (see pp. 408-410), decided to be the first person to leave the sinking *George M. Cox*. With him in a lifeboat he took a single female passenger. The *Cox's* captain ordered him back, commanding that he fill the lifeboat. First mate Cronk, a practical man who evidently thought he would be stranded on the small island for some time, loaded his lifeboat with 17 people, all women.

George Cox, the ship's nurse, and three of the injured boarded a steamer which had responded quickly to the call and took them to Port Arthur. Meanwhile, the Rock of Ages lighthouse keeper and his wife scrambled to make room for 116 unexpected guests on their tiny, barren rock island. The 116 lined the crowded spiral staircase of the lighthouse, while many men took turns standing outside in the cold. All sipped coffee vigorously. The next day, the cutter, *Crawford*, removed the guests from their cramped quarters and returned them to Houghton, where they lodged at the Douglas House, the town's best hotel.

Thar she blows! All 121 people on board the GEORGE M. COX *on her first voyage under her new name were removed to safety. The ship stuck like a stranded whale on Rock of Ages Reef at Isle Royale in 1933.* GREAT LAKES MARINE COLLECTION OF THE MILWAUKEE PUBLIC LIBRARY/WISCONSIN MARINE HISTORICAL SOCIETY.

Subsequent salvage operations on the *Cox* removed the guests' personal property and all retrievable machinery, fixtures, and equipment, including two cars and the ship's safe. An inquiry placed most of the blame upon first mate Cronk, who had been placed in command for about three hours that afternoon and who, according to the charges, had changed course slightly. The captain, however, was clearly in command at the time of the fog-shrouded impact, yet he avoided shouldering the brunt of the responsibility. What became of first mate Cronk after this, his second Lake Superior shipwreck, is not known.

Not until October, 1933, did the *Cox* break in two and disappear.

Built in 1901 at Toledo, Ohio, as the *Puritan* by the Craig Shipbuilding Company, this 1,762-gross-ton steamer serviced mostly Lake Michigan ports until 1918, when the U.S. Navy bought her for use as a troop transport and training ship in World War I. She returned to Lake Michigan in 1919 for transportation work until 1930, when the Great Depression mothballed the vessel at Manistee, Michigan. She was there when George M. Cox purchased her.

The *George M. Cox* is the second-most visited shipwreck at Isle Royale, topped only in popularity by the nearby *America*. The steel remains of the *Cox* lie broken and scattered in two underwater gullies on the same kind of hard rock that stranded the ship in 1933. The bow pieces lie in 10' to 20' of water, scattered around a 250' radius. Of greater interest, the stern lies in 40' to 100' about 150' east of the bow section. The *Cox's* hull broke just forward of the four boilers, which lie exposed on the hard bottom. In spite of this jumble of rubble, visiting divers will be ultimately impressed with this historic shipwreck.

Diver Gary Gentile swims in and out of various passageways among the boilers and other steel debris of the steamer, GEORGE M. COX. PHOTO BY CRIS KOHL.

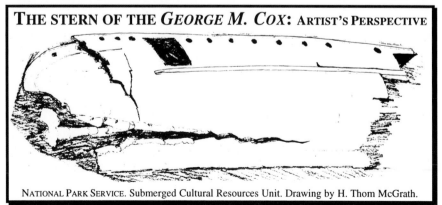

THE STERN OF THE *GEORGE M. COX*: ARTIST'S PERSPECTIVE

NATIONAL PARK SERVICE. Submerged Cultural Resources Unit. Drawing by H. Thom McGrath.

Diver Don Edwards descends the marker buoy line directly above the stern of the shipwreck, GEORGE M. COX, *with its several boilers.*   PHOTO BY CRIS KOHL.

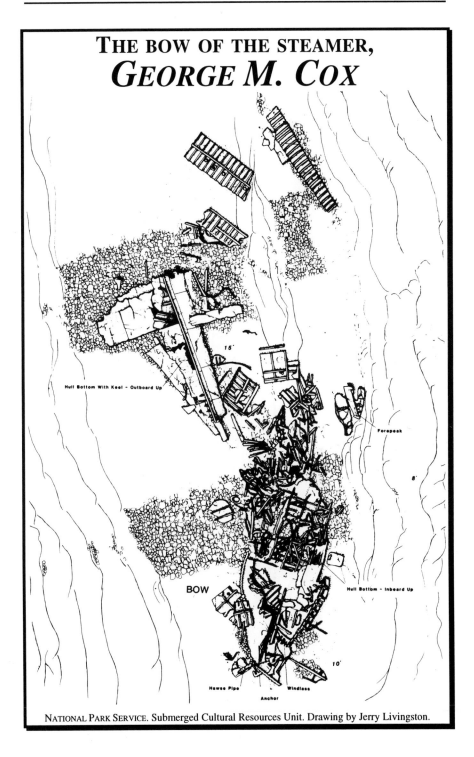

THE BOW OF THE STEAMER,
GEORGE M. COX

NATIONAL PARK SERVICE. Submerged Cultural Resources Unit. Drawing by Jerry Livingston.

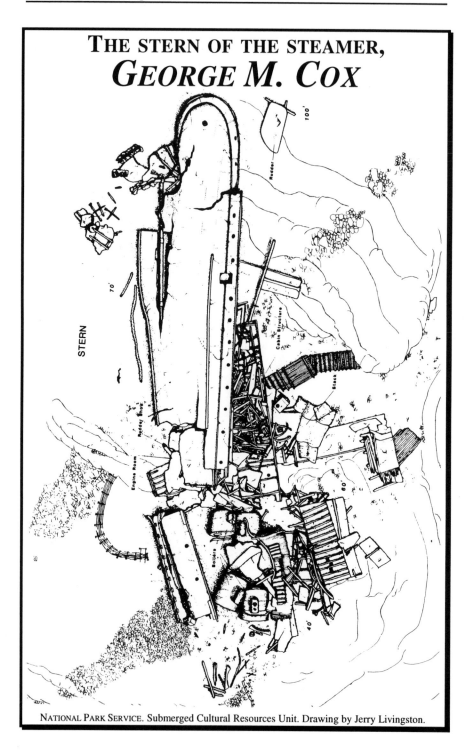

THE STERN OF THE STEAMER,
GEORGE M. COX

NATIONAL PARK SERVICE. Submerged Cultural Resources Unit. Drawing by Jerry Livingston.

Ely, Samuel P. (#8 on the map on p. 355)

VESSEL NAME:	SAMUEL P. ELY (also S.P. ELY)
RIG:	three-masted schooner; later schooner-barge
DIMENSIONS:	200' x 31' 6" x 13' 8"
LAUNCHED:	1869; Detroit, Michigan
DATE LOST:	Friday, October 30, 1896
CAUSE OF LOSS:	stranded along breakwall
CARGO:	none (in ballast)
LIVES LOST:	none (from 10 on board)
GENERAL LOCATION:	along west breakwall in Agate Bay, MN
DEPTH:	20' - 35'
ACCESS:	boat
DIVING SKILL LEVEL:	basic
DIVING HAZARDS:	boating traffic
CO-ORDINATES:	Lat/Lon: along the inner west breakwall
	Loran: halfway between shore and the light

The three-masted, 200' schooner, *Samuel P. Ely*, built in 1869 at Detroit, Michigan, by J.P. Clark, was launched as the *Florence*, but was renamed prior to her enrollment on August 3, 1869, at Cleveland, Ohio. This 627-gross-ton ship toiled as a marine workhorse for almost 30 years, hauling mainly coal and iron ore between Cleveland and Lake Superior ports. Her value steadily decreased, ranging from $27,000 in 1875 to $10,000 in 1895, and requiring repairs in 1879, 1882, 1886, 1887, 1889, and 1894. The *Ely* sailed the inland seas as a schooner, under her own sail power, but she was reduced to a barge in 1887, spending her final nine years demoted to the cut-down status of a schooner-barge being towed around the lakes by a steamer. She almost ended her career when a heavy gale stranded her on Drummond Island in Lake Huron on Sept. 13, 1894, but she was recovered and repaired at a $1,000 cost.

The *Samuel P. Ely's* final voyage began when she was towed by the tug, *Hesper*, from Duluth to Two Harbors, Minnesota, on October 30, 1896. Severe seas extended the two-hour trip to nine hours. The *Hesper* lost courage in "the highest seas in memory," dropped the *Ely's* line outside the harbor, and "steamed safely in," leaving her consort at the mercy of the 50 mile-an-hour winds. The crew of eight quickly dropped her anchors, but the powerful winds made them drag. The *Samuel P. Ely's* final voyage ended when she was pounded against the inner (northern) side of the west breakwall. The two-man crew of a small scow, also stranded there, jumped aboard the larger vessel. The *Ely's* hull broke during the buffeting and the ship sank at 3:00 A.M. The ten men were rescued from the rigging the next morning by the tug, *Ella G. Stone.*

The SAMUEL P. ELY *in tow in a Great Lakes harbor.* GREAT LAKES MARINE COLLECTION OF THE MILWAUKEE PUBLIC LIBRARY/WISCONSIN MARINE HISTORICAL SOCIETY.

The almost intact schooner, *Samuel P. Ely*, is reportedly the most popular shipwreck site on Lake Superior's north shore. Sitting on sand in 35' of water, and rising about 15' off the bottom, this shipwreck is easily penetrated because of missing hatch covers and broken bow and stern ends. Wooden railings and the deck, with occasional whisks of white paint still discernible, plus a bilge pump and winch, greet visiting divers. The Ely's stern is next to an ancient stone breakwall, while a mast lies off to one side. Fish life usually abounds here. Recreational scuba divers recovered the ship's bell in November, 1990, coming into conflict with the state's recently enacted shipwreck legislation. The bell went to the Lake County (MN) Historical Society, which restored and displayed the artifact at the Two Harbors Museum, Lighthouse Point. The *Ely* must be reached by boat, as private property surrounds the site. A buoy or breakwall paint usually marks the location of this shipwreck.

Emperor

(#9 on the map on p. 355)

VESSEL NAME:	EMPEROR
RIG:	steel bulk freighter (steamer)
DIMENSIONS:	525' x 56' 1" x 27'
LAUNCHED:	Sat., December 17, 1910; Collingwood, ON
DATE LOST:	Wednesday, June 4, 1947
CAUSE OF LOSS:	stranded
CARGO:	iron ore
LIVES LOST:	12 (from crew of 33)
GENERAL LOCATION:	Canoe Rocks, eastern Isle Royale
DEPTH:	30' - 130' (slopes to 175')
ACCESS:	boat
DIVING SKILL LEVEL:	intermediate-advanced
DIVING HAZARDS:	depth, hypothermia, penetration, silting
CO-ORDINATES:	Lat/Lon: 48.12.39 / 88.29.47
	Loran: 46150.6 / 31711.8 (bow)

A major Lake Superior disaster occurred early in the morning of June 4, 1947, when the 525' steel steamer, *Emperor*, hit hard on the Canoe Rocks, filled with water, and sank with her bow just awash in the shallows, and her stern deep in 175' of water. Twelve lives were lost in this needless accident.

The Canadian ore freighter, *Emperor,* had loaded 10,429 tons of iron ore at Port Arthur, Ontario, and pulled away from the dock at 10:55 P.M., June 3, 1947, underway towards Ashtabula, Ohio. First mate James Morey, who had spent long hours supervising the ship's loading at Port Arthur, took command of the ship at midnight during her dark zigzagging past various islands, points, and shoals towards the open, clear waters of Lake Superior.

At 4:45 A.M., the *Emperor* crashed into the jagged Canoe Rocks with the force of a locomotive slamming into a wall. The hull cracked, admitting an enormous volume of water and causing the stern to sink in deep water off the pinnacle of the rocks, and also trapping the men in the engine room.

Captain Eldon Walkinshaw and 11 crewmembers went down with the ship, but, miraculously, the 21 others on board survived. The U.S. Coast Guard cutter, *Kimball,* happened to be placing channel buoys around Blake Point on the other side of Isle Royale. When she received the S.O.S. from the *Emperor*, the *Kimball* raced to the accident scene in 25 minutes, rescuing seven survivors from their precarious position on the tiny Canoe Rocks, which rise a meager three feet above the water, plus 14 more from two lifeboats that were so damaged they would not have stayed afloat much longer.

The immense 525' steamer, EMPEROR, *was nicknamed "The Pride of Canada" because, at the time, the ship was the largest ever built there.* GREAT LAKES MARINE COLLECTION OF THE MILWAUKEE PUBLIC LIBRARY/WISCONSIN MARINE HISTORICAL SOCIETY.

The accident was difficult to explain. The three people who could possibly have offered some answers, Captain Walkinshaw, first mate James Morey, and the wheelsman at the helm, had all perished in the disaster. Not one of the 21 survivors had any idea why their ship veered off course. A Canadian Court of Investigation concluded that Morey was not as alert as he could and should have been, and that there was a strong possibility that he dozed off and was thus delayed in making one of the required course changes. That error put the *Emperor* too far south, right on course with Canoe Rocks.

The Canadian Court also disapproved of the "system which prevailed which required the first mate to be in charge of loading the ship during the period when he should have been off duty, and resulted in his becoming overtired, suffering as he was from lack of sleep." Also criticized were insufficient lifeboat drills, as the crews did not seem to be familiar with their stations and duties.

In 1910, at the time of her launching at Collingwood, Ontario, the steel steamer, *Emperor*, was the largest ship ever constructed in Canada. Her enormous length and load capacity were complemented by the 2,200 indicated horsepower triple expansion steam engine, soon earning her the nickname, "The Pride of Canada." In the end, the insurance company paid out $632,700 for the loss of the *Emperor*, which was owned by Canada Steamship Lines.

With her radio mast and support cables barely above water, and her pilot house awash, the EMPEROR *made a tragic picture the day after the wreck.*   AUTHOR'S COLLECTION.

Although the *Emperor's* hull split, the halves are still somewhat attached, forming a long line of massive, cracked, chipped, breached, and fractured steel dropping from a depth of about 30' at the bow to 175' at the bottom of the propeller. Do not even think about exploring this entire wreck on one dive or from one end to the other. It's too dangerous with such an enormous shipwreck. That's why the Isle Royale National Park Service usually places two separate, distinct, and distant marker buoys on this wreck, one at the shallow bow and the other at the deep stern. The most distinctive and interesting sights at the bow are the anchors and the large, open holds, in water 30' to about 80' deep. The descent line to the deeper stern is usually positioned to drop the diver at about the 115' level of the wreck. The deckhands' quarters were on the stern's forward port side, in about 120' of water, replete with bunkbeds still in place. The ship's galley is a bit deeper. Most doors are open or absent, providing that degree of safety during an aquatic exploration. The *Emperor's* stern railing sits at 150', with the propeller in 175' of water, but this is deep diving. Exploring the *Emperor's* stern, even if you don't go deeper than 130', is a serious dive requiring careful adherence to a logical, cautious dive plan. Do not descend deeper than 130' unless you are highly trained and experienced.

The *Emperor,* the magnificent ship that died in dreadful horror with tragic loss of lives, retains a silent, eerie mystique that compels every visitor to feel at least a tinge of restless apprehension when exploring her fragmented, shadowy remains.

THE WRECK OF THE EMPEROR

ARTIST'S PERSPECTIVE

NATIONAL PARK SERVICE. Submerged Cultural Resources Unit. Drawing by Jerry Livingston.

ABOVE: *The deckhands' quarters are situated at a depth of about 120' in the stern section of the* EMPEROR. *Bunkbeds still stand against the walls, while open drawers still contain clothing.* BELOW: *Diver Gary Gentile, determined to try his hand at some underwater cooking, explores the contents of the* EMPEROR'S *galley. Utensils and supplies have been set on a galley stove.* PHOTOS BY JOYCE HAYWARD.

Howard

(#10 on the map on p. 355)

VESSEL NAME:	HOWARD; launched as D.D. PORTER
RIG:	wooden tug
DIMENSIONS:	114' 5" x 22' 2" x 10'
LAUNCHED:	1864; Philadelphia, Pennsylvania
DATE LOST:	Monday, June 13, 1921
CAUSE OF LOSS:	stranded
CARGO:	none (in ballast)
LIVES LOST:	none (from 14 on board)
GENERAL LOCATION:	Victoria Island, near Thunder Bay, Ontario
DEPTH:	45' - 120'
ACCESS:	boat
DIVING SKILL LEVEL:	intermediate-advanced
DIVING HAZARDS:	depth, hypothermia, darkness, remoteness
CO-ORDINATES:	Lat/Lon: Location is described on next page.
	Loran:

This wooden U.S. gunboat, built in 1864, outlived most of the people that were born that year. Launched as the *Admiral D. D. Porter* at Wilmington, Delaware, on salt water, this 114' 5" ship was issued its first enrollment at Philadelphia on November 21, 1864.

Over the course of the next 57 years, this vessel was owned at an eclectic list of places: Chicago, Cleveland, Buffalo, Quebec, Sarnia (Ontario), Port Huron (Michigan), Ashland (Wisconsin), Duluth (Minnesota), and West Bay City (Michigan). The ship changed owners and ports of call liberally, bouncing from one Great Lakes country to the other, then back again. She was rebuilt at Kingston, Ontario, in 1882, and again at West Bay City in 1904. We know that her name was changed to *Howard* in 1889, and that she ended her long career running out of Fort William, Ontario, under U.S. registry and ownership.

With background vagaries similar to those of a riverboat gambler, the *Howard* did manage to make some headlines in her life before her demise. At noon on November 27, 1888, the *Howard* (still named the *Admiral D.D. Porter* at this point in her life, but under Canadian registry), caught on fire at Port Huron, Michigan, and burned off her upper cabins. The $3,000 damage was covered by insurance. After this rebuild, her ownership and name were changed. On May 11, 1895, the tug, *Howard*, then owned by W.H. Singer of Duluth, collided with the barge, *Odin*. The barge's injuries were minimal, but the *Howard's* forward hull damage required $300 to repair.

The tug, HOWARD, *lived its life under different names, many owners, and a multitude of locations, including both salt and fresh water. Always on the go, the ship was rarely photographed.* REV. PETER VAN DER LINDEN COLLECTION.

In heavy fog on June 13, 1921, the *Howard* ran aground on the reef at the southwest end of Victoria Island near Fort William, Ontario. The first mate took the lifeboat, rowed west to Cloud Bay, and struggled through the forest and underbrush to highway 61, where he caught a ride into town. He procured a tug which headed to the *Howard's* rescue. The *Howard*, however, sank after being pulled off the reef. No lives were lost, and the tug was too old to salvage.

To visit this site, take a boat three miles from Cloud Bay, or a bit further from Little Trout Bay, to the SW point of Victoria Island. The wreck lies on the north side of the reef, the side facing the mainland, almost mid-distance between the 59'-tall tower light on the point and the spar buoy marked "M7." Follow the 45' contour out from the point of land.

The *Howard's* engine, two boilers, smokestack, and propeller sit on a gravel ledge at a depth of 50' to 70'. Considerable portions of the wooden hull remain at this site, with the bow section considerably broken and scattered. There is quite a bit of this shipwreck in deeper water to 120' below the boilers. Reportedly a wrecked barge lies at 90' to 100'. In 1962, local scuba divers recovered the *Howard's* whistle, now in the Thunder Bay, Ontario Museum. Visibility at the site is usually excellent, and the wreck is quite photogenic.

Kiowa

(#11 on the map on p. 355)

VESSEL NAME:	KIOWA
RIG:	steel freighter (steamer)
DIMENSIONS:	251' x 43' 6" x 22' 2"
LAUNCHED:	Tues., May 18, 1920; Wyandotte, Michigan
DATE LOST:	Saturday, November 30, 1929
CAUSE OF LOSS:	stranded
CARGO:	grain (flax)
LIVES LOST:	4 (from 23 on board)
GENERAL LOCATION:	off Au Sable Point Lighthouse, Michigan
DEPTH:	25' - 35'
ACCESS:	boat
DIVING SKILL LEVEL:	novice-intermediate
DIVING HAZARDS:	hypothermia, penetration (limited)
CO-ORDINATES:	Lat/Lon: 46.38.71 / 86.13.21
	Loran: 31499.78 / 47425.19

The steel steamer, *Kiowa,* emerged from the emergency shipbuilding program which the U.S. government began in World War I to replace saltwater vessels being sunk by U-boats on the Atlantic coast. While over 300 ships were built under this program, World War I ended before some of them, such as the *Kiowa,* were finished. Their construction was completed by private funding.

Finally sliding down the launch ramp on May 18, 1920, at the yards of the Detroit Shipbuilding Company of Wyandotte, Michigan, as hull #286, the *Kiowa's* completion was financed by the Independent Steamship Company of Detroit. This 2,309-gross-ton, steel steamer measured 251' in length, 43' 6" in beam, and 22' 2" in draft. Her 1,250 horsepower triple expansion engine and two Scotch boilers were brand new when they were lowered into the *Kiowa's* hull during construction. The *Kiowa,* built with four watertight bulkheads, a double bottom, and four large holds, was a duplicate of six other ships from that yard.

In March of 1927, after seven years of work hauling package freight and limited bulk cargo, the *Kiowa* was sold to the O.W. Blodgett Company, of Bay City, Michigan. Ironically, under this new owner, the *Kiowa* experienced her first major problem when, on July 23, 1927, she stranded hard on a rocky reef in foggy weather near Parisienne Island in Whitefish Bay. The seriousness of the damage can be assessed from the $30,000 repair bill!

The *Kiowa* was shipping a cargo of flax seed from Duluth to Chicago on November 30, 1929, when a fierce early blizzard coated her with thick ice.

With this topheaviness came a shift in the cargo, and water flowed into the listing hull. The boiler fires were extinguished and the *Kiowa*, with 23 men on board, drifted helplessly before the seas somewhere west of Grand Marais, MI.

Contracted to the government to be built for service on the Atlantic Ocean during World War I, the 251' KIOWA was completed by private enterprise when the end of the Great War removed her need as a national necessity. AUTHOR'S COLLECTION.

Captain Alexander T. Young, owner O.W. Blodgett's son-in-law, frantically took to a lifeboat with ten of the crew. When their boat quickly capsized in mountainous waves, six were yanked back onto the *Kiowa*, one dragged his way back into the lifeboat (he was later found frozen to death in the bobbing boat), but the captain and three others drowned. Newspaper accounts first praised the dead captain's courage, before the less noble truth came out. Mate Arthur Cronk, of Detroit, who was now in command of the doomed ship, managed to calm the remaining crew. By the next day, the *Kiowa* was stranded on a reef near shore. Two deer hunters, Earl Howay and Charles Chilson, took their launch to the distressed ship and removed a load of men (including First Mate Arthur Cronk, who lived to survive yet another shipwreck, see pp. 392-398) to the Au Sable Lighthouse, then returned for the rest, which they had on board when the Grand Marais Coast Guard boat finally arrived. The hunters turned their cargo of sailors over to them. In their report, the Coast Guard gave themselves credit for rescuing all of the survivors, an issue quickly contested by the two hunters in the press. The Coast Guard ship, however, did remove all 18 rescued men to Grand Marais.

The *Kiowa* soon broke up, but some tackle and deck machinery was salvaged. The ship's cargo of flax seed became fish food, noticeably increasing the local aquatic population of whitefish, which local commercial fishermen shipped down to Chicago because the fish tasted too much of linseed oil.

This shipwreck lies four miles west of the Au Sable Point Light, about 1,200' directly off the west side of the middle stairway to the beach at Twelve

Mile Beach campground. Most of the shipwreck, in large sections 40' to 80' long, is still on site, in spite of the natural ravages of ice, wind, and waves which helped break her up, and the salvage of some of her metal during World War II. The largest chunks of the *Kiowa* sit in about 30' of water and can usually be seen from the surface on an average day, since they run a high profile.

The KIOWA *stranded off the Au Sable coast, this calm scene after the storm belying the violence in nature which killed five of the ship's crew.*   AUTHOR'S COLLECTION.

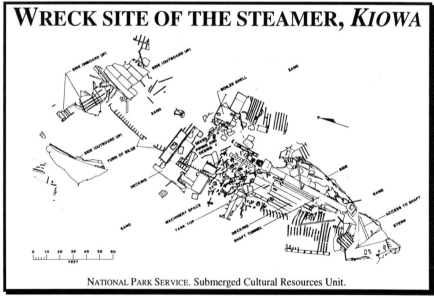

WRECK SITE OF THE STEAMER, *KIOWA*

NATIONAL PARK SERVICE. Submerged Cultural Resources Unit.

Langham

(#12 on the map on p. 355)

VESSEL NAME:	LANGHAM; launched as TOM ADAMS
RIG:	wooden steamer
DIMENSIONS:	281' 1" x 41' 4" x 20'
LAUNCHED:	Tues., April 24, 1888; West Bay City, MI
DATE LOST:	Sunday, October 23, 1910
CAUSE OF LOSS:	burned
CARGO:	coal
LIVES LOST:	none (from 16 on board)
GENERAL LOCATION:	off Bete Gris Bay, Keweenaw Peninsula
DEPTH:	90' - 106'
ACCESS:	boat
DIVING SKILL LEVEL:	intermediate-advanced
DIVING HAZARDS:	depth, silting, hypothermia, remoteness
CO-ORDINATES:	Lat/Lon: 47.22.37 / 87.55.53
	Loran: 31758.1 / 46675.8

The cool, deep blue waters of Lake Superior sing a siren's song to scuba divers sweating at the stern of a dive boat on a hot summer day, fully suited and geared up just prior to taking this comfortingly refreshing dip for a visit to the remains of the steamer, *Langham.*

Visiting divers will easily find this site, since local divers usually place a white jug on this wreck every springtime. The *Langham's* two boilers, engine, and machinery are in place in their original locations, with much of the ship's hull still intact, although the superstructure, including the decks, burned off just prior to the sinking. Visibility is usually in the 25' to 35' range, although excessive rainfall for two or three days prior to a visit can reduce the visibility at this site to somewhat less.

Of course, there is much more to any shipwreck exploration than just eyeing ship's parts. Knowledge of the vessel's demise will make this aquatic visit all the more interesting and enjoyable.

The *Detroit Free Press* of Tuesday, October 25, 1910, reported the loss of the steamer, *Langham,* thusly:

WOODEN FREIGHTER BURNS AND SINKS OFF KEWEENAW POINT

"Calumet, Mich., October 24 --- The second disastrous wreck within a week off Keweenaw Point, Lake Superior, [author's note: the earlier one was the brand new 580-foot steamer, *William C. Moreland,* which broke in half on Sawtooth Reef off Eagle Harbor, Michigan, on October 18, 1910; the stern half was salvaged and rebuilt into another ship] occurred Sunday when the large wooden steamer, *Langham,* owned by John I. Adams, Detroit, coal laden, bound from Cleveland to Fort William, Ont., burned and sank six miles off Betegris [sic].

The wooden steamer, LANGHAM, *launched as the* TOM ADAMS, *caught fire and sank in a little over 100 feet of water just off the east side of the Keweenaw Peninsula on October 23, 1910. No lives were lost in this accident. The* LANGHAM *had served the Great Lakes for 22 years.* GREAT LAKES MARINE COLLECTION OF THE MILWAUKEE PUBLIC LIBRARY/WISCONSIN MARINE HISTORICAL SOCIETY.

"The steamer is a complete loss and it is unlikely any attempt ever will be made even to salvage her engines. After burning seven hours the steamer sank stern first in 120 feet of water. Her crew of 15 with Captain John H. Sinclair, Port Huron, and one woman, the wife of the cook, escaped in two yawls and viewed the sinking of the *Langham* from a distance of a quarter of a mile. Some of the crew narrowly escaped death in the flames which spread rapidly and burned into the vessel's deckload of hard coal. Few of them saved their personal effects.

ABOVE: *The marker buoy indicating the resting place of the steamer,* LANGHAM, *is usually attached to the top of the shipwreck's triple expansion engine.* BELOW: *Burbot, also called ling, lingcod, and "lawyer fish," are seen on most Great Lakes shipwrecks, including the* LANGHAM. *Shunned as a fish-food, burbots predaciously feed upon smaller fish and may reach four feet in length.* PHOTOS BY PETER TOMASINO.

"The fire was discovered at 7 a.m. and the steamer burned to water's [sic] edge, sinking at 2:30 p.m. Her boilers did not explode, the safety valves having been opened when the crew left the ship after having fought the flames hopelessly for five hours.

"The *Langham* encountered heavy storms Friday and Saturday this side of Whitefish Point. She ran behind Keweenaw Point off Betegris [sic] Saturday afternoon for shelter from the northwest gale and anchored six miles off shore. Her anchors were down when the fire was discovered and the flames prevented the crew from raising the hooks or slipping the chains and running the steamer on the beach to save her engines and hull.

"Captain Sinclair and his crew left this evening for Detroit to report to the owners.

"When she was built at the yards of F. W. Wheeler & Co., in West Bay City, in 1888, the *Langham*, then known as the *Tom Adams*, was the largest wooden vessel ever turned out in Michigan. She was 281 feet long, with 41.4 feet beam and 20 feet deep. Her gross tonnage was 1,810 and she had a carrying capacity of 3,000 tons of iron ore.

"After the new steel steamer *Thomas Adams* was built in 1902, the wooden steamer's name was changed to *Langham*. She was valued at $40,000 and insured for $30,000. Her coal cargo of about 2,800 tons, is estimated at about $100,000."

The *Langham's* engine was a triple expansion type built by the Cleveland Ship Building Company in 1888 and capable of producing 850 horsepower, while her two Scotch boilers were constructed by the same company in the same year. When launched, the vessel had two black stacks with a wide white band and a black ball on each (later reduced to a single smokestack), four masts with topmasts and later two pole spars.

At her first inspection on April 28, 1888, the *Tom Adams* (renamed *Langham* in 1902) was appraised at $120,000 and rated A1, the best possible category for insurance purposes. Her identical sister ship was the *Robert L. Fryer,* which was built in the same year at the same place by the same company as the *Langham*. The *Fryer* shared the same fiery demise as the *Langham*, but the *Fryer* was purposely torched as a public spectacle off Fort William (now Thunder Bay), Ontario, in the summer of 1930. The *Fryer* is also a popular scuba dive site today.

The *Langham's* first enrollment was issued at Detroit, Michigan, on May 3, 1888; her final enrollment was surrendered at that same harbor on March 31, 1911, five months after she burned and sank.

Reportedly on October 25, 1983, a ship fouled the wreck of the *Langham* and brought up a four-ton folding stock anchor with about 250 feet of chain on it. The anchor was moved to Eagle Harbor, Michigan, where it was put on public display. A post or pre-dive visit to the anchor would certainly be in order for a full appreciation of the *Langham* shipwreck site. Have fun!

Madeira

(#13 on the map on p. 355)

VESSEL NAME:	MADEIRA
RIG:	three-masted schooner-rigged steel barge
DIMENSIONS:	436' x 50' 2" x 24' 2"
LAUNCHED:	1900; Chicago, Illinois
DATE LOST:	Tuesday, November 28, 1905
CAUSE OF LOSS:	stranded
CARGO:	none (light; in ballast)
LIVES LOST:	1 (from 10 on board)
GENERAL LOCATION:	Split Rock Point, Minnesota
DEPTH:	30' - 110'
ACCESS:	shore or boat
DIVING SKILL LEVEL:	intermediate-advanced
DIVING HAZARDS:	depth, penetration, hypothermia
CO-ORDINATES:	Lat/Lon: 300' off shore, buoyed
	Loran:

A Duluth newspaperman wrote, in the summer of 1955, that "skin divers" from the Frigid Frogs dive club were finding that Lake Superior's floor is an underwater scrap yard, and that the hull of the *Madeira* "looked like it had been worked over with a can opener," but two anchors still hung from the bow.

He wrote: "The 'treasure' aspect of the *Madeira* is nil. Nothing remains of her after cabins and wheel house. The lake floor is littered with broken plates and all the divers got for their trouble was a brass porthole wingbolt and a lot of fun...."

Times and attitudes have changed a lot since 1955. Just when spearfishing divers on the West Coast gradually saw their fish supply thinning drastically, so Great Lakes divers in the 1970's and 1980's witnessed their unique shipwrecks being pilfered to nothingness by every underwater visitor wanting to take home a souvenir. But unlike the ocean fish, historic shipwrecks are nonreplenishable. Legislation has been passed and education has been put into place to protect both West Coast fish and Great Lakes shipwrecks.

The *Madeira* was picked to pieces while awaiting such protection. In less heritage-conscious times, a hardhat diver named John B. Wanless, according to the DULUTH HERALD of August 12, 1915, "...brought to this port today a lighter [a lighter was a boat used for salvage or unloading] load of scrap iron from the wrecked steamers *Lafayette* and *Madeira*.... Mr. Wanless is just now taking what iron and other parts of the wreck are most valuable and bringing them to Duluth for disposal." Forty-five years later, that attitude towards shipwrecks had not changed. On July 29 1960, a company named Schwalen-Opheim Corporation reportedly purchased the rights to the *Madeira* from the Pittsburg Steamship Division, U.S. Steel Corporation [the *Madeira's* last owner], for the purpose of salvage. A *Madeira* anchor was raised and sold to the nearby Split Rock Trading Post by that salvage company. Divers in 1960 also removed the ship's wheel, which also ended up on display at the same establishment. In 1974, it was reported that, due to rising scrap metal prices, a wrecking crew worked all summer on the *Madeira*.

The huge steel barge, MADEIRA *(1900-1905), carried three masts and a steam engine for hoisting sails and raising anchors.* GREAT LAKES MARINE COLLECTION OF THE MILWAUKEE PUBLIC LIBRARY/WISCONSIN MARINE HISTORICAL SOCIETY.

Historically, the young *Madeira* took on Superior, and the lake won. The 436', 5,039-gross-ton steel barge, launched at Chicago in 1900, was in tow of the steamer, *William Edenborn*, on November 28, 1905, when the ship was stranded and broken against a cliff near Split Rock Point in one of the worst storms in Great Lakes recorded history (several other ships were also total losses). One life, first mate James Morrow, was lost from the ten on board the *Madeira* when he fell from the mast while trying to climb to the top of the cliff.

The *Madeira* basically lies broken in three sections. The bow, in 40' to 50', is upside-down, while the stern, with its large steam winch and open hatches, lies on its starboard side in 65'. A small, roofless pilot house sits at 75'. The entire wreck is fascinating to explore, in spite of its torn apart look.

ABOVE: *The* MADEIRA, *one of the most popular dive sites in Lake Superior, offers views of ship's bitts, open hatchways, and hawsepipes where the anchors once hung.* BELOW: *Open hatchways allow a look inside the huge hull. This dive can be done from shore. Half a mile north of Split Rock Lighthouse, follow a trail to a gravel beach with a scenic view of the lighthouse on the right, and Golden Cliff on the left. The buoy marking the* MADEIRA'S *bow is under Golden Cliff.* PHOTOS BY JOYCE HAYWARD.

Mesquite

(#14 on the map on p. 355)

VESSEL NAME:	MESQUITE
RIG:	Coast Guard cutter (buoy tender)
DIMENSIONS:	180' x 37' x 14'
LAUNCHED:	Saturday, November 14, 1942; Duluth, MN
DATE LOST:	Mon., December 4, 1989 and July 14, 1990
CAUSE OF LOSS:	stranded and scuttled
CARGO:	none (other than buoys))
LIVES LOST:	none (from 53 on board)
GENERAL LOCATION:	off Keweenaw Point, western Lake Superior
DEPTH:	82' - 112'
ACCESS:	boat
DIVING SKILL LEVEL:	advanced
DIVING HAZARDS:	depth, penetration, silting, hypothermia
CO-ORDINATES:	Lat/Lon: 47.22.38 / 87.55.55
	Loran: 31714.6 / 46712.8

It was 2:30 A.M. on December 4, 1989, when the ship lurched and the nightmare began. The *Mesquite* had hit rocks off the Keweenaw.

The Keweenaw is a large peninsula which juts northward into Lake Superior from Michigan's Upper Peninsula. It is basically a wilderness area known for its numerous copper deposits. The Keweenaw is one of Michigan's underwater preserves because of its high concentration of shipwrecks.

The *Mesquite* was a U.S. Coast Guard buoy tender, 180' long and constructed of steel by the Marine Iron & Shipbuilding Company of Duluth, Minnesota, in 1942, at the peak of World War II. Her total cost by the time she was commissioned August 27, 1943, was $894,000. The ship's twin diesel engines propelled her at 13 knots, and her cruising range was an incredible 30,000 miles. From 1944 until the end of the war a year later, the *Mesquite* served in the Pacific, including a stint in the Philippines, sailing with the Seventh Fleet. After the war, the *Mesquite* was stationed at Sault Ste. Marie, Michigan, until 1959. Then she worked out of Sturgeon Bay, Wisconsin, until 1977, and after that until her demise, from Charlevoix, Michigan. The *Mesquite* made occasional forays further afield, including the seizure of a drug ship in the Caribbean in 1985. Later that year, the *Mesquite* unloaded machine guns and ammunition at Traverse City, Michigan, for transfer to another Coast Guard vessel heading for drug patrol off Key West. The *Mesquite* herself spent her final winter afloat, 1988-89, cruising the warm waters off Key West on drug patrol.

ABOVE: *The 180', steel Coast Guard buoy tender,* MESQUITE, *pictured in about 1960, was 47 years old when she stranded and became a total loss in late 1989.* INSTITUTE FOR GREAT LAKES RESEARCH, BOWLING GREEN STATE UNIVERSITY, OHIO. BELOW: *The first part of the* MESQUITE *to come into clear view is usually the railing at the uppermost portion of this shipwreck, seen in this 1991 picture taken a year after the* MESQUITE *was scuttled in 112' of water.* PHOTO BY CRIS KOHL.